FACING THE SHARDS

Joy Ruth Mickelson

Published by FYD Media, LLC
www.fydmedia.com
ISBN 10: 0989163474
ISBN 13: 9780989163477
LCCN: 2015956550
FYD Media, LLC

Dedicated to my Family
Without whom this Memoir would not have been written.

ACKNOWLEDGMENTS

To the published authors: Eunice Scarfe, who encouraged me to share my story; Pierrette Requier, Edmonton Public Library Poet Laureate, who listened and taught me how to listen; Margaret MacPherson; Becky Blake; Friends in Academia-Jean D. Clandinin; Pam Steeves; Vera Caine, and Florence McKie, my first writing partner in 1962. All the writers know the power of story. My grateful thanks to my editor Laurie Stevens, who shared her wisdom, and my Copy Editor Monica O'Rourke.

CONTENTS

GLOSSARY

balabusta	a good housekeeper
bureikas	pastries made of flaky dough; cheese, meat, or veggie filling
challah	braided bread loaf especially used on Sabbath
cholent	a slow-baked dish of meat, beans, and potatoes
coke	a fuel with few impurities, usually made from coal
nisht	not
plotz	to burst, explode, overcome with emotion; to faint
Shabbos	the Jewish Sabbath, which begins at sundown on Fridays
schlemiel	an unlucky, awkward, or stupid person
schlep	to haul or carry; a tedious journey
schmoozing	to chat in a friendly and persuasive manner
schul	synagogue
tallis	prayer shawl
traif	non-kosher
vorsht	kosher salami
Yom Tovs	Jewish festival days

Prayer:
"Shema Yisroel Adonai Elohenu Adonai Echad."
"Hear, O Israel, the Lord is our God; the Lord is one."

CHAPTER 1
COUNTRY LIFE IN THE WEST

"Ah yes. Jews. You're the people who don't believe in God."
The headmistress's bold statement became a legend in our family. It was 1934, and I was four years old when she said that to my mother. My sister, Viv, was two years older. You had to be six to start school, and she was eager to enrol. We three were huddled outside the headmistress's door.

A shiny brass plate on the front of her office was engraved "Miss F. Burchill, BA Oxon."

She opened the door and pointed to a chair. "Sit."

When this story, coloured by passing years, was told to friends, Mum said she had refused to sit. "What amazed me most was that her degree was from Oxford University. Her ignorance shocked me. I wondered what they taught her about world religions at that famous place. I told her we Jews brought monotheism to the world, that Christ was a Jew, and that there would be no Christian religion had it not been for the Jews."

Mrs. Baum, one of Mum's oldest friends, queried, "Raie, what did she say to that historic list?"

"She appeared dumbfounded," Mum said. "I think most of the villagers found her forbidding. And she was. She held her nose high in the air, and when she spoke, her lips curled. It looked like a sneer to me, but it might have been the beginning of a sniff. I don't expect anyone had dared answer her the way I did."

Things sorted themselves out that morning. Miss Burchill allowed Viv to be placed on the first-class register. I followed two years later when I turned six. I was in the first class only one year when we moved again. Back to London.

When Dad had originally decided that we needed to come to the village and leave the city, he had given his reasons. "We'll do better in the West Country. I can't make a living here however hard I work. It's the newest suburb of London, and our deli is losing money every week. There aren't enough Jewish families here who keep kosher. The partners want out. Times are against us. The Depression is taking its toll. To top it all, Raie, d'y'know what the insurance agent said to me today when I went to renew our policy? He had the nerve to say, 'We haven't had good experiences with your kind.' Then he insinuated there would be a fire at the shop 'of unknown origin'."

Mum soothed him and reminded him that we'd dealt with prejudice like that all our lives and had survived. "I'll make sure we'll fit in, Mark. You'll travel in three counties with your new company, you'll get to know customers in out-of-the-way places, and I'll make friends with the neighbours. Iris-Vivienne and Joy can join Brownies and play with the locals, and the fresh air will do us all good."

My sister didn't like the name Iris-Vivienne. So I called her Viv.

Three years passed. We did fit in, in a way, to that place where we were the only Jews. Mum never complained. She always had a smile on her face, although some of the local customs caused her smooth forehead to wrinkle. The one that bothered her most was when the church people came to the door. "It interrupts my reading!"

They came every week to try to convert us. They stood on the front step talking for hours. If the wind blew, they moved into the porch to shelter. But they wouldn't come inside our house. Mum would offer them a cup of her favourite Assam tea, but they always refused.

We couldn't understand why. Perhaps they thought we might convert them?

Dad asked, "Don't they know Jews don't believe in proselytizing?"

We'd never heard that word before. Dad made the meaning clear to Viv, and Viv tried to help me understand. I was probably the only seven-year-old in the West Country who half-understood what it meant.

When I thought about it later, I realized that although we'd had good times, we didn't fit in tightly—like fingers in a leather glove. Our good times were always with ourselves.

Early every morning, Mum, Viv, and I picked wild mushrooms in the fields at the bottom of our garden. We had to avoid the cow pats scattered around, although we did occasionally slide on one or two. Whenever this happened, I laughed, Viv moaned, and Mum groaned. She knew how hard she would have to rub the scrub board—up and down, up and down—to remove the yellow stains from our ankle socks.

After we climbed back over and under our barbed-wire fence, trying not to get our jerseys snared by the pointed barbs, Mum rushed to make our breakfast. We had to hurry. We dared not be late for school. If you were, a large red mark was placed by your name on the daily register, and you were given a ten-minute detention.

At breakfast, the mushrooms sizzled as they fried. They smelled of the fields and the sun and the sizzling sound tickled our ears. We would add two large brown-shelled eggs to Dad's breakfast plate because he was always hungry at the end of the day when he came back from his travelling work. He appreciated our scouring the fields for mushrooms and thought highly of eggs with brown shells.

Mum said that with our wide grins we looked like the Bisto Kids, except we weren't wearing coloured hats, and our clothes weren't patched. The Bisto Kids' faces were everywhere, advertising the popular gravy mix. Mum wouldn't use it because it wasn't kosher, but she liked the posters.

Once, our village school had a Fancy Dress party, and Mum sewed our costumes. We were exact replicas of the Bisto Kids. Viv was the girl and I was the boy. I wore trousers and had braces to hitch them up. Viv had coloured stockings. We won second prize. Dad thought we should have been first.

Before the Fancy Dress Parade, Miss Burchill made another odd remark. "I didn't know you could sew such fancy costumes, Mrs. Abrahams."

That evening Mum asked Dad, "What did she think I was? A complete *schlemiel*?"

"You're oversensitive, my dear. She hasn't made the time to get to know you."

Mum felt better when he said that. Dad knew how to soothe her.

Mum sewed all our clothes except our woollen vests and knickers. She sewed our summer dresses and winter dresses, our summer coats and winter coats and hats. She never used a pattern. She designed everything in her head. She let us choose the material we liked but had the final say, in case the fabric was too thick and wouldn't sew well on her Singer treadle. She knitted whatever we needed: pullovers with no sleeves, and cardigans with buttons down the front, long white socks and short coloured socks. Mum sewed kilts for the three girls who lived next door. Their father had died suddenly, and they were all sad. We liked them, and I think we could have become firm friends, but the next month they moved to be near their grandparents in Northern Scotland and we never heard from them again, even though they promised to write.

We held our breath when Dad came home from his travels. Two weeks was a long time for him to be away and we missed him. He was interested in history and would tell us about where he'd been and what he'd seen after he'd finished work for the day. He liked stately homes and famous historical sites. He described the Stone Circle at Avebury. Immediately we asked him to take us to Wiltshire. We wanted to run in and out of the tall standing Circle Stones. He promised he would but said that I had to grow taller first. I wasn't sure why. He also told us the names of places that made us laugh. He called Moreton-in-the Marsh "Slopton-in-the-Slosh." He had visited it during a rainstorm, and his shoes, socks, and trousers had been soaked by the downfall.

"Do you think Dad is strict?" Viv asked me one evening as we were washing the supper dishes.

"Yes," I answered, "sometimes I do. I hate it when he shouts, 'Which of you two girls has left her jammy fingers on the light switch?'"

Viv laughed. "I think he's said it five times this week. 'Are you sticking your fingers in the jam pot, Joy?'"

"'And why aren't you pulling the chain, Viv?'" We doubled over, our tummies creased. We had an old-fashioned lavatory, and Dad would yell, "You girls, what did I tell you? Pull that chain!"

"I think Dad wants us to be like sisters who never quarrel," said Viv.

"That might be difficult," I replied. "The other day I heard the Phelps triplets fighting and screaming at each other in the grocer's shop. Let's not be like them. I do love you, Viv," I said as I gave her a friendly slap on her backside. She returned the words and the compliment.

Dad came into the kitchen at that very moment. "You girls quarrelling again?" His voice was angry.

How mistaken grownups can be, I thought.

"Dad, didn't you and your brothers quarrel when you were boys?" Viv asked.

A look of remembrance surfaced on Dad's face, and he smiled as he pointed to a family photo with a crooked face inside its frame. "We boys were nine years apart. Your uncle Isidore was the oldest, Uncle Lewis the youngest, and I was in the middle. My brother Izzy bossed me: 'Do it this way. No! That way. Mark, don't be a *schlemiel*.' One *shabbas* your grandma asked me to put the cutlery on the table. Izzy removed every single piece of cutlery I had placed. I was highly annoyed, picked the largest grapefruit I could find in the fruit bowl, and threw it at him.

"He ducked. It hit your great-aunt Sophia's photo and there she remains, crooked as ever. Your grandpa was angry with me, not with Izzy, the favoured one, and caned me with his thin willow cane."

That was my father. He could be full of surprises: stern one minute, loving the next. Once, when he had been away travelling for two and a half weeks, he surprised us. "Gather up your glad rags. We're going to stay with Mrs. Lovelace for five days."

Dad used funny phrases like "glad rags" when he was in a good mood. We laughed loudly.

We wanted him to stay in that good mood.

"Who's Mrs. Lovelace?" we asked. "Does Mum know her?"

"I stayed at her cottage last week. I'm not going to tell you more, but I know you'll love it. She has her own little path that winds down the cliffs to the beach. It's not easy, but I think you two will manage. Wear your strong shoes—plimsoles will slip on wet cliffs, and the sea spray can travel quite high."

We gathered our things while Mum made sandwiches for the journey. Dad's work had loaned him a car that he was allowed to use on weekends as long as he didn't overdo it. On the way, he told us about Mrs. Lovelace and her thatched cottage; how she liked girls and she liked Jews; how she liked singing and country dancing; how she could make scones that melted in your mouth; and how excited she was about meeting us. We couldn't wait to meet her. Viv asked Dad to tell us about thatched roofs—how they were made, what happened if there was a fire, and how they kept the rain out. Viv was learning about Medieval England at school, and the way she spoke, I think she knew more than Dad.

The car was having a struggle. The lanes were twisty, narrow, and steep and the engine made popping noises. "It's exhausted," said Dad.

Suddenly I blinked.

Down, down, down in the far distance was the sea, shimmering blue with crusty white caps.

"Won't be long before we're there, cooling our hot bodies." Mum reassured us.

I hoped I'd be able to float on my back and look up at the sky. Mum floated on her back easily. She said saltwater helped keep you up and that even though she was so fat, she would never sink in the sea.

We arrived at the cove. Near the shoreline, the seawater gentled into white foam. Beyond its bubbles, the water's colour darkened to a deep blue. We swam and swam and floated and floated. We splashed each other with large scoops of water. We had piggyback races, me on Mum's back and Viv on Dad's. When we were tired, we stretched out on the sand. Mum and Dad took forty winks. Viv and I whispered secrets together. The car had had a good rest too and was no longer making popping noises as we continued on our journey.

We were still sleepy when we arrived at Mrs. Lovelace's thatched cottage, but even through half-closed eyelids I could see it was like a painted picture postcard. The thatch was dark brown and looked like witches' brooms without the handles—the twigs were packed together so tightly. The front door was framed by an arch and a shrub with flowers woven in and out. Mum said it was called Clematis Jackmanii and was very special. It had grown in the West Country since 1863. Its rich deep purple inspired Dad to burst into his best singing voice, "When the deep purple falls over sleepy garden walls ..."

I wanted to bury my face in the softness and beauty of the clematis. I touched its petals, and they felt like tissue paper.

The flowers in Mrs. Lovelace's rock garden were all the colours of the rainbow. She must have been the hardest-working gardener in the West Country. Mrs. Lovelace reminded me of a fairy godmother. She was tiny. I was sure she could make any wish I had come true.

She had magic in her fingers and her smile.

My eyes were getting tired and Viv and I were ready for bed. Our fairy godmother took us up the twisty, narrow staircase to the attic room that was all whitewashed and smelling of lavender. A huge feather bed filled the room, and we thought we were lying on a cloud until the feathers bunched together. Viv showed me how to pummel the bunches down and make the feather mattress level and smooth. We had to be careful not to bump our heads on the ceiling, which came to a steep slope by the window. Without moving our heads from the bolster pillow, shaped like a sausage, we could see to the end of the back garden.

I whispered to Viv, "I think there are fairies at the bottom of the garden."

Viv was already asleep. I hoped I'd remember to ask her tomorrow. The sheets smelled of sunshine and were as white as daisies. I fell asleep. I didn't hear the creaky stairs when Mum and Dad came up to kiss us good night.

Our life continued. We stayed at Mrs. Lovelace's cottage twice more. It was perfect each time. She danced with us on the sand holding our hands, swinging our arms and singing. We learned every verse of "Come Lasses and Lads Take Leave of Your Dads and Away to the Maypole Hie." She promised to take us to see the villagers dance the Maypole, but we never got the chance.

CHAPTER 2
A MOONLIGHT FLIT

We were busy at school, and Mum and Dad were pleased with our report cards. We laughed when we saw our class photos. Viv had her eyes closed, and I was beaming like a Cheshire cat. I looked foolish. None of our London relatives came to visit. It was too far and cost too much money. Neither Viv nor I were prepared for what happened next: we did a moonlight flit to London.

It was only years later that I knew what those words meant. When Dad used them then, Viv and I started to giggle. "We're moving back to London. It's a secret. You girls can't tell anyone. Mum's the word."

We giggled again. "Flit! What a funny word."

Dad frowned.

In bed, Viv and I whispered. We decided we'd miss some people here. I would miss my playmate Johnny Heath, and we would both miss Mrs. Lovelace, but London had museums and art galleries that Mum and Dad had visited. The idea of being in the same city again as our grandparents and relatives was exciting. Aunty Phyllis was Viv's favourite aunt, and Viv said she would enjoy visiting her. Viv often told me about Aunty Phyllis's fake bulldog. His fur was real and his face was lifelike. There was a chain by his head, and when you pulled the chain his mouth would open and he would let out a ferocious roar. I could hardly wait to see such a lifelike bulldog.

We both understood that what we were going to do would take place in the evening. It was winter and the moon came up early; it might happen after our suppertime or even late at night, well past our bedtime.

Viv thought the word flit came from fly. "I'm not sure," she said. "It could come from flee."

I didn't want to flee and told her so.

The week before, our house was turned upside down. Our possessions were packed into boxes of many shapes and sizes. We couldn't take all our furniture or the gardening tools. Dad's spades and hoes and wheelbarrow would have to be left behind. We wouldn't have as much space in London. I wondered why not. I was glad Mum took her favourite wooden spoons and jelly moulds, and I hoped our London kitchen would have a large pantry with enough shelves to hold Mum's pickled onions and borscht.

When our flitting did occur, something out of the ordinary happened. We went to the cinema. We'd only been to the cinema three times before. There we were, Mum, Viv, and me at six o'clock in the evening, watching a film called *Captain January* starring seven-year-old Shirley Temple.

We were sitting in the balcony on seats Mum said were the most expensive in the cinema. The seats were comfortable and so soft and plushy that my eyes were drooping and every few minutes I nodded off.

Viv kept poking me. "Don't miss this part. It's funny."

Suddenly a lady with a torch flashed it along all the rows in the balcony and called out in a loud, important voice, "Mrs. Abrahams. Mrs. Abrahams."

Mum jumped up. "Usherette! That's me!" Mum sounded worried, and as we followed her down the stairs, we were also worried.

Uncle Leon stood at the bottom of the stairs.

Mum cried, "What's happened? Has there been an accident? Is Mark safe?"

Leon said, "Quickly. Outside. In you get, girls. The Rover's comfy in the backseat. Raie, the front seat should be wide enough for you. It's off to London we go."

I could have punched him for insulting Mum. I crossed him off my "favourite relative" list.

There had been no accident. Dad was at the driving wheel of the Rover, and Mum's tears and worries changed into smiles of relief. Between them they bundled us into the car and away we went. Dad revved the engine and drove off at full speed. "Keep your eyes on that lorry ahead. It's carrying our goods and chattels. Uncle Leon's with the driver and will show him the way to Mater's flat."

Dad called his mother "Mate".

"Mater means "mother" in Latin, but we call her Mate, for short!" He told us.

Viv and I still called her Grandma Hal. We were glad we would be seeing her more. I wondered whether she knew we were fleeing.

Dad's voice came from the driver's seat. "You girls try to go to sleep before we get to Mate's. It'll be a long journey." A loud snore came from the front. Mum's snore.

The night was clear and the moon shined brightly. The tree trunks and hedgerows threw shadows that made the countryside look different. Magical. Sparkly. I never questioned why we left in such a hurry. Neither Viv nor I knew Dad couldn't earn enough for the four of us to survive. He tried in the nearby towns but couldn't find another job. We had to forfeit all we owned: our house, our piano, our wardrobes. We left owing money to the milkman, the baker, and the green grocer.

Mum felt ashamed. "One day I'll go back and make amends."

The opportunity never arose. I'd hoped I would never have to do a moonlight flit when I grew up.

Our journey felt endless, and I dozed on and off.

Suddenly, Viv poked me. "Look out the window. All I can see now are streets and streets, rows and rows of shops, and no fields. See the railway bridge on the other side? I think that's near Aunty Nettie's dress shop.

"Can you can find her sign 'Jean Jay'? She's been there more than ten years. Grandma Hal's flat is on top of the shop, and I'm convinced we'll be happy staying with her until Dad can find us another flat. We'll be squashed together in the four bedrooms, and as usual, Grandpa Louis will complain. I know he will."

When we arrived, just as we had predicted, we heard his moany, grouchy voice: "We're going to allow you to stay here. I expect you children to behave yourselves." Grandpa Louis had silvery, wavy hair. He would pat it and stroke it while he sat in his most favoured leather armchair.

Dad would whisper, "Vanity. Vanity. All is vanity."

"Now then, Mark, he is what he is," Mum said.

"Whatever does that mean?" Viv asked me.

"I think Dad is mocking Grandpa Louis. Mum closes all discussions about family members with an emphatic: 'You are what you are!'"

Grandma Hal said to us, "Vivienne, you and Joy will have to sleep in the attic, but limit your talking, as your cousin Derek is studying for his exams in the small alcove next to you."

Derek was our favourite cousin. He was seven years older than me. He was our hero. He was funny and kind, and always welcomed us with a joke. His favourite chestnut was, "Why did the chicken cross the road?" He studied at a big oak desk with more compartments and pigeonholes than any desk I'd seen before. We wanted him to succeed in his exams and enter the well-known grammar school nearby.

It would be *Pesach*, or Passover, soon, a festival of freedom, and Viv and I were thrilled to be celebrating the *Yom Tov* with so many of our family. Derek always helped the family at Passover by carrying the foods we ate to the small kitchen in Grandma's flat. Our glass Pesach plate had special containers for the foods that were symbolic of the story of the Exodus: parsley for spring; grated horseradish for our bitter tears; a shank bone for the paschal lamb; *charoset*, a chopped mixture of nuts, honey, and cinnamon represented the mortar that held the pyramids together when we were slaves in Egypt; and a hard-boiled egg symbolized life.

As well as this precious plate, other relations who came to celebrate with us had cooked their favourite dishes: Aunt Phyllis, Derek's mum, roasted a large turkey; Great-Aunt Tilly chopped the liver, eggs, carrots and onions; Uncle Lewis brought the unleavened bread called matzah. Matzah contained no yeast. (There had been no time for the dough to rise during the Exodus from Egypt.) The brisket, baked by Mum, smelled delicious, and the crowning odour was chicken soup.

"Mate always makes the chicken soup for Pesach. It's the tops!" Dad declared as he pretended to slurp a large spoonful.

To get to Aunty Netty's shop from Grandma Hal's flat you had to go down three flights of twisty stairs. On the front floor facing the street was her showroom. In the room behind sat two seamstresses, each with her own Singer treadle. They worked tirelessly all day, altering dresses that were too tight for a customer, shortening those that were too long, and pressing and steaming wrinkled hems. They were loyal to Aunty Netty and had been employed by her for more than twenty years. They greeted Passover as if they were Jewish themselves and knew all the prayers and songs.

Family members would come and go through the shop while Aunty Netty was trying to run a business. "There's too much traffic here!" she would declare in an irritable voice.

Another difficulty for Aunty Netty was that she was short of storage space for her stock. The new dresses had to be placed in boxes on the narrow ledges going up the stairs. The previous Passover, as Derek was carrying Mum's brisket, he tripped on his untied shoelaces and dislodged a box from the shelf, spilling the meat and gravy over four expensive silk dresses. There were groans upstairs and downstairs.

At our first Pesach together living in Grandma Hal's flat, Derek helped me to learn Hebrew and say the *Ma Nishtana*, the question asked during Passover: "Why is tonight different from all other nights?" These were traditionally sung by the youngest child at the Seder, the Passover meal. When the time finally came for me to chant the *Ma Nishtana*, I was able to remember neither the tune nor the Hebrew words he had taught me.

I was mortified.

What a relief I felt when I heard Derek's voice covering my silence. He gave the answers to the questions and explained that on this night we ate matzah and bitter herbs dipped twice in saltwater, and we ate in a reclining position to show we were no longer slaves.

It made me realize how squashed we were living together. Finding enough pillows to recline upon for the Passover meal was difficult enough. There were too many of us. Dad knew we had to find a place of our own. He needed to work, but jobs were scarce. We had been staying with Grandma Hal for many months. The cooking was tiring her and Grandpa Louis continued his moaning. The crowded living continued to be a difficulty for Aunty Netty. We liked being with our grandparents and aunt but realized we might have been a burden.

CHAPTER 3
NOT YET GENTRIFIED

The house Dad found for us at 131 Brondesbury had seen better days.

"It looks scruffy," Mum said, "inside and out."

Mum told us those better days were in 1905 when she was a girl. She had lived on the next road, Victoria Terrace, and her family— our Grandma Marie, Grandpa Henry, and Mum—had the whole house to themselves. They were well off then, with two maids and a cook. Those days were gone. Grandma Marie was said to have gambled away a small fortune playing poker.

My family history and the marriages were complicated. It was easy to get muddled up. Grandma Marie was married to Grandpa Henry, who was my step-grandpa. He was also my father's cousin. We were connected on both sides.

Grandma Marie was small and not particularly kind. Grandpa Henry was tall, had a ruddy complexion, a big red moustache, and a fat tummy. He was in leather goods and owned a store that sold trunks and cases. They weren't well off now. None of us were. We were a working-class family. Our mum and dad played card games with us, took us on picnics to Greenwich Palace with our sandwiches wrapped in brown paper bags, took us swimming in the Vale of Health on Hampstead Heath, and took us rowing on the River Thames near Sunbury Lock almost every weekend. Our father's mother, Grandma Hal, smoked cigarillos and told jokes. No one else I knew had a grandma who smoked and made them laugh. It's true we did have an aunty and uncle who had three dogs and a big house in the country, but as Dad said, "They didn't put on too many airs and graces."

Our branch of the public library was around the corner from our new house. Mum and I went every few days with a pile of books in our shopping bag. It was so close to where we lived that it was like having a library in our home. One day, as she was stamping our loan cards, the lady at the desk said to Mum, "She's a regular little bookworm, isn't she?"

I grinned.

Three families lived in 131. Our family name was Abrahams, and the four of us had the three-room flat on the ground floor—flat number one. The Isaacs had three rooms on the second floor in flat number two, and Miss Jacobs had the two rooms on the top floor, flat number three. The flat numbers and the names were written in ink under the push bells. The ink ran when it rained, and it was difficult to see the names clearly. Dad joked we lived with the Patriarchs—Abraham, Isaac, and Jacob.

Miss Jacobs was kind to us and sent us picture postcards when she went on holiday. She said the stairs made her huff and puff too much and she wished she lived on the ground floor. We were glad we slept in the front room, right by the front door. Mum and Dad had given us that room because the sun shined brightly through the huge Edwardian windows. Their bedroom was next to ours, and it was dark and never caught the sun. Dad said they didn't mind not having the sun and that we needed sunlight to grow big and strong.

Everyone came in by the front door. We had to be careful not to go into the front hall in our vests and knickers because nothing separated the three flats. I didn't want anyone from flat two to see me in my nightie. Anybody could be in the front hall. We could hear loud voices, loud music, and all the loud coughs and sneezes. It was awful in the winter. The coughing and sneezing went up and down, as if we were tossing wheezes back and forth, each floor catching colds from the other. We all hated it.

We couldn't hear those noises in our third room, which we called our Everything Room, because it jutted out from the back of the house and had its own low roof. Nothing was built on top of "everything." To get there you had to go down three steps at the back of the front hall, along a passage, past our bathroom and lavatory, our cellar where the coal was kept, and our side door. Mum called our Everything Room dismal, but at least we could light the fire. The chimney sweep had to come every year. The amount of soot that he swept down with his brushes surprised us all.

Viv and I used to pirouette in front of the fire, warming ourselves. We twirled and twirled until we were dizzy.

"You girls will get chilblains if you get too close!"

"Not us. We spin too fast," we replied cheekily.

The bedroom Viv and I shared was cramped. Our two beds took up most of the room, with only enough space left for a chest of drawers. There was a marble mantelpiece over the fireplace, but we never lit a fire in that grate even though we shivered and froze when we undressed.

Despite the cold, we had lots of fun in our room. Every night in bed we would sing to each other or recite our favourite poems. Viv knew all the verses of "Cockles and Mussels" and "Loch Lomond." I used to make her laugh when I recited the poem "Abou Ben Adhem" in a religious voice.

When Mum and Dad weren't home, we would dare each other to go round the room. The rules were: your feet were not allowed to touch the floor, nor could you step on the mattresses. The bed frames, top and bottom, were thin and hard on the soles of our feet, but the chest of drawers was an easy climb. The hardest part of the game was climbing on the marble mantelpiece. It was narrow and up high. It was very difficult to flatten yourself against the wall and walk on the ledge without falling. I never managed to "do the marble."

Our new school friend Katy could. She was skinny and a good runner and climber. She won our "round the room" game every time.

The old Singer sewing machine, with its squeaky treadle, was covered with a huge wooden hood. The Singer was Mum's pride. We liked playing with the treadle pedal, pushing it with our hands to make it go up and down as fast as we could. The Singer's wooden hood was perfect for our games. We used it as a boat, Viv, Katy, and I. We would squeeze in together rocking furiously, singing in raucous tones, "What shall we do with a drunken sailor, what shall we do with a drunken …" and would rock ourselves right out of the upside-down cover and fall giggling onto the floor.

When the weather was warm, we played in the back garden. Viv and Katy preferred to play "round the room" in our bedroom, so I would play in the backyard by myself. It was a thin perpendicular shape, with a bump where the scullery interfered with its straight lines. There was a brick wall all the way round the garden, high on one side and the back, and low on the other side. The bricks were a greeny-grey colour and looked like mildew. They were dirty and old, and the wall had crumbled in several parts. Dad said the mortar had died. I hadn't known mortar could live and breathe. Dad tried to explain, but it was too technical for me.

The buildings all round us were eight storeys high, with shops on the bottom and flats on top. Our house only had three storeys, so everyone could see me if I played in the back garden. I hated that. We had one advantage. A trunk. A huge, bent-over, scumbly, weathered tree trunk.

It belonged to a twenty-foot poplar tree. You could climb the trunk until it reached our wall, and then you had to stop. All the branches and leaves were in somebody else's garden.

Once, one of our neighbours complained that our trunk was pushing on and wrecking their wall. Dad said it was our wall. It became a real shouting match.

Dad stood his ground.

The man sneered, "You Jews are all the same. Think you own everything."

"Ignorant sod," Dad huffed as he retreated into the scullery.

In the end we all lost the wall. It crumbled later during the war after a bomb fell.

In the back garden lived my favourite pet. He wasn't the only pet I had before the war, but I loved him the best. I say *he* but he may have been a she. I didn't give him a proper pet name. I called him what he was: Tortoise. He was very large and round and had a shiny shell with sharp, definite patterns that were not always visible. I would take my magnifying glass to peer closely at his beauty. Mum said he must be a hundred years old. I thought he could scamper very quickly for a hundred-year-old tortoise.

Mrs. Sofaer, our next-door neighbour, said he was the biggest tortoise she had ever seen. "And I know turtles. My young nephew went to South America and sent me photos of turtles laying their eggs."

I wasn't sure what the difference was between a tortoise and a turtle, and I didn't know Mrs. Sofaer had a nephew, but I hoped I could go to South America one day.

Tortoise loved lettuce. I would sit on our trunk and offer him lettuce, and when his head popped out, I would stroke it softly and gently. The time would go by in flash, and I never tired of feeding him. The triangular shape of his little head made me feel happy inside, similar to the way I felt when I held the Bantam chickens we had when we lived in the West Country.

Viv wouldn't feed him or stroke him. "I don't like creepy, crawly things," she said with a shudder.

I tried to sing his praises, but it didn't work. She couldn't stand spiders either. I tried to help her hold a spider in her hand once, but she screamed and shook it onto the ground. It quickly scuttled away. Spiders' lacy webs intrigued me, especially in the early morning if there was dew on them. I would stare at the lacy webs for hours. I remember our teacher had once told us a story at school about a king who was inspired by a spider's determination. It helped the king fight his enemies.

There was a boy in my class called Phillip Friedman. He and I were the only two Jewish pupils in the class of forty. Phillip and I raced neck and neck for first place in all our subjects. It was hard to squeeze between the desks if you were called up by the teacher to read in front of the class, or explain how you had solved an answer to a sum. Phillip's wire spectacles were always crooked. They would slip halfway down his nose, making him peer over them. Some of the class called him "Professor Phillip." He didn't mind. He could explain problems as well as the teachers. His hair was a mess. It looked like a floor mop.

"Tidy that hair, Phillip." "Tell your mother to take you to the barber." "Put a rake through that crop." Those were comments the teachers made.

I didn't think teachers should make remarks like that to Phillip.

We'd been friends for two years at school, but I didn't want him to kiss me or anything like that. I was only ten years old. I'd never been to his house. Mum said we lived in the poor end and his parents were probably well-off. They were Orthodox Jews. Our great-grandparents had been Orthodox, but now we were middling and assimilated.

One Monday evening in June 1939, as we were finishing our supper, our front doorbell rang. Dad went up to the front hall. He called down, "There's a young gentleman here for you, Joy, with a present."

Viv was home. "Your boyfriend's here, Joy. Run up, he's come to kiss you!"

She always teased me about boys.

Phillip looked small; his grey socks had slipped round his ankles, and his short grey pants hardly reached his knees. His yellow moustache gave him away—he'd had an egg for supper.

I was surprised that Phillip was at the front door. He was holding something covered with a tea cloth.

He whipped the cloth off like a magician. Two twitchy rabbits were sitting there. One white and one a tawny colour.

"These are for you, Joy. I am leaving for America. I shall miss Whitey and Browny. You can keep the cage. I shall miss you too."

He thrust the rabbits and their cage into my dad's arms and ran, waving his hand and mouthing "G'bye."

We stood there. Speechless.

Then we both started laughing.

My laughter almost turned to tears. I thought I knew why he was going to America. Viv and I had overheard Mum and Dad talking seriously every night. There had been rumours of war for more than a year. Our uncles had spoken about atrocities that had happened to Jews in Germany. Viv and I had discovered a book Dad had hidden in a chest of drawers. It had pictures of undressed Jewish women: back, front, and side views. Their bodies were badly bruised and damaged. They had been severely beaten. It was horrible to look at. Viv read the page and told me it was true. The German Secret Police were responsible for those brutal acts. The date of the book was 1936. I hoped it would be safer for Jews in America.

In the end, I only had Whitey and Browny for one month. Whenever I could, I would stroke and cuddle them. Even Viv enjoyed unlatching their cage and holding one of them in her arms. You had to be gentle. And if you put your face on their fur you could feel their little hearts beating. I was careful to divide my time fairly. I didn't want Tortoise to feel left out.

Dad said I had to be in charge of cleaning out the rabbits' cage. Having never kept rabbits, I was surprised by how much they ate and how many pellets came out of their bums.

"Things are heating up, both here and in Europe. We're not sure what's going to happen. I'm sorry, Joy. The rabbits will have to go."

"Where, Dad? Where?"

"I'll take care of it. I *am* sorry. I know how fond of them you both are."

When bad things happened, they happened quickly. Before I could turn around, Whitey and Browny and their cage had disappeared. It was as though they had never been in the garden. Dad wouldn't tell me where their new home was, but I didn't have a good feeling about it. Mum hadn't liked the rabbits' smell, but she tried to make me feel better.

"I took a snapshot of them with my box Brownie. I'll put the picture in our family album. I know you'll like it."

I didn't like the blurry snapshot. Everything seemed to be in the shadows, and Browny looked black.

I wondered if Phillip would miss his rabbits.

I hoped he would write to me. I knew I would miss him when he left.

CHAPTER 4
REMEMBER SEPTEMBER

I awoke to the quick click-clack of my mum on the treadle of the Singer sewing machine.

I opened my eyes carefully. The treadle cover sat right way up, on the lino, and my mother was feeding burlap sacking into the foot lifter.

"Mum, what time is it?" I whispered, glancing at Viv's bed.

She was awake too, sitting upright, her black hair framing her pale, thin face.

"Shhh … go back to sleep … it's morning already, and I'll soon be done."

My fears couldn't get out of my mouth fast enough. "But Mum, what *are* you doing? Where's Dad? Is it morning? What is that?"

"I'm sewing new haversacks … for your clothes to go in … you'll see … and I've bought you both some new vests and knickers."

Her words came out tightly, through her stretched lips, as she tried not to lose the sewing pins she had stuck there.

I knew my mum. I felt her fears and they mingled with mine, but the only words that whined out were: "We don't need new vests and knickers. Do we, Viv? Ours are perfect. They've got no holes, and the elastic isn't stretched."

Deep inside I knew.

I'd read the papers. I'd heard the words.

Bombing. London. Hitler. War.

"Send the children away." "They'll be safe in the country." "Evacuate all children from London."

I half-whimpered, half-groaned, "But I don't want to go away! I don't want to go into the country! I don't like the country! I want to stay here with you. So does Viv, don't you, Viv?

"I'll be good, ever so good. I don't mind if you have to go to war work. I'll cook, I'll do the shopping, I can light the copper boiler by myself, you know I can. But we won't be in the way. No! I don't like other people. I don't … I don't like the smell of their homes. I don't care if they're kind. I don't want them to be kind.… No! I don't want to be safe. I don't care if the bombs come. I don't care if I'm killed. *I want to stay with you! I want to stay ho … o … ome!*"

Viv threw a book of poems at me. "Stop whining—you're making things worse. We can't stay if the war comes. You're nine years old. Act your age!"

I stopped. I wondered how other nine-year-olds in London were acting.

The next day at school our teacher handed out gas masks and two labels to everyone present. The labels were luggage labels made of pale, thin cardboard with a brown hole at the top. Two thin bits of white string were threaded through the hole.

Our teacher said, "Tell your parents to write your names and addresses on both of these labels *in big letters* and bring them back to school tomorrow. They're to be tied onto you. On the front of your chests. Don't forget! And get your parents to help you with your gas masks so you can put them on quickly when the air raid warning goes. We don't want a repeat of what happened here today, do we?"

Chaos—that's what had happened! The chaos of thirty-six eight- and nine-year-old boys and girls practicing putting on smelly, rubbery, twisty, ugly gas masks for the first time.

The hard wooden, iron-footed desks at which we usually sat uniformly two-by-two squeaked and screeched when they were moved to make room for us to gather round our teacher.

I thought the noise would break my eardrums. I was afraid. Everything smelled peculiar.

When Dad came home, I whined again like I had when Mum was sewing our haversacks. But even as I was protesting, I knew they had made up their minds.

However painful this was, it had to be done.

"Stop being soppy!" Dad said sharply.

I knew I had to stop.

British girls were not supposed to be soppy even if they were Jewish as well. I hadn't been very British that evening. The previous hour had been horrible, trying to breathe in that stinking gas mask. I felt suffocated and couldn't get any breaths. I thought I was going to die.

Viv put her mask on, took it off, and put it on again. It didn't seem to bother her.

"Look at Iris-Vivienne. See how she does it," Dad said proudly.

I tried to copy her. But I couldn't. I thought Viv was only pretending that she didn't mind. Mum didn't seem to understand how scared I was. She had that look on her face of "try harder." The same look as when I missed a catch when Dad threw spin balls at me.

"Well, we'll have to hope they don't use gas in this war," Dad said.

Mum was cross. "That was cruel, Mark. Tell Joy you didn't mean it."

Dad said he was sorry and was only trying to joke and make me laugh.

I burst into tears.

I didn't cry on Friday, September 1, 1939, the morning we were sent away.

We lined up two-by-two, labels tied to our coat buttons and gas masks hanging diagonally across our chests, their long straps making a steady *boink boink* as the boxed masks banged our knees. When we marched up to the station bridge, the curbs were lined with grown-ups shouting "Hurrah."

"You brave littl'uns."

"You'll be safe in the country."

"Don't forget us now! Have a cuppa for me."

I looked back and saw Mum and Dad standing on the corner of our street, but they couldn't see me. I saw my mum turn her face into Dad's chest. My own chest hurt.

We tried hard to be brave those years we were away. We never let on. We were never "soppy." We never told them our stories; we kept a "stiff upper lip" because "there's a war on."

We never told of that first day: the long train journey, the school getting split, separated, and us boarding the wrong train and arriving at the wrong place—a place where we weren't supposed to be and where nobody was expecting us.

Our teachers had tried to keep our spirits up. We sang "Ten Green Bottles" over and over, until I had to put my hands over my ears. I knew I'd never want to sing about those bottles again. We arrived at a railway station, and the teachers said, "Well, those six hours have gone by quickly." I didn't know how they could think it was quick. The six hours felt like twenty-six hours to me.

We followed the teachers out of the station and onto a gravelly side road and walked and walked and walked until we came to a church with a tall spire. Viv and I had never been in a church before, and we weren't sure if we ought to enter it. But some helping ladies patted our shoulders and made us move into the dark and dusty church hall. I thought it couldn't have been used for years. Hungry and tired, we were given huge bars of chocolate. Most of us had never seen ones that size, so we tucked in. The combination of dirt, dust, and chocolate was overwhelming. Only those with cast-iron bellies stayed in; the rest of us rushed to the field outside. It was horrid, and dark, and everyone was being sick everywhere. Dark outside and dark and smelly inside. I wanted the whole day to vanish. I wanted to vanish too.

I tried to pretend I wasn't there, that nothing was happening.

But it *was* happening, and I *was* here, in the present, startled by sharp, loud hand clapping.

"Outside! Outside! Line up in straight lines! Brothers and sisters together! Hold hands. Hurry! Hurry!"

Viv and I held hands and were near the beginning of the straggly line of nearly 150 children. Even the bouncy boys had lost their bounce. The helping ladies said they were billeting officers. Viv told me a billet was the place you were put and that it was somewhere you would have to stay until the war was over. The billeting officers wandered amongst us asking questions and writing things on bits of paper. It was long past my bedtime. It had been twelve-and-a-half hours since we left London, and I shut my eyes and pretended I was back with Mum. I could barely whisper. They asked Viv and me to give our names, to say whether we had any brothers or sisters with us, and to tell them our ages and our religion.

It all felt strange. The helping ladies banged the door knockers. Doors opened and dim hissing gaslights cast shadows that looked like birds with sharp beaks. It was so different from the lights we had in London. It made the faces of the grownups who came out of the doorways yellow and ghostly. "Was that a man?" I couldn't tell. Perhaps it was a lady, but in the dusky dark and with their yellowy green faces, it was hard to decipher. Some of the grownups came outside with their children. The children stared at us.

They looked us over like we were things to buy.

They took their time.

Some grownups pointed with their fingers: "I'll take those."

One lady pointed with a walking stick.

Others stood in their doorways and yelled, "Give me two boys!" or "I can only take one."

The line got shorter and shorter; the boys and girls from our school were disappearing around us. A big boy in front of me shouted, "Take me. Take me."

And he was taken. Everyone was being chosen.

Suddenly, a voice boomed behind us.

We jumped.

"What? These two? Oh! These two are Jews!"

"Of course we're Jewish," I whispered to Viv. "What difference does that make? Why won't anyone take us in?"

Viv whispered back, "Let's tell them we're English too. I'll tell them it's only a religion. I'll tell them that Christ was a Jew. Let's recite the poem 'How odd of God to choose the Jews. But not so odd as those who choose a Jewish God yet spurn the Jews.'"

But we couldn't do it. We were too frightened to stand up to them and too sick for home to do anything. We heard our teeth chattering. The helping ladies banged hard on more doorknockers.

Their voices echoed through the shadows. "Will you take those two standing over there? They're Jews. They seem to be nice little girls. I don't think they'll give you much trouble."

Another lady shouted louder, "Could you take these two small girls in? But I must tell you, they're Jews. Please take them. It's very late. They're tired and we're very tired."

We were left to the last of that 150 straggle. The helping ladies whispered in clusters. We realised they didn't know what to do with us. Then it happened.

A front door opened wide, and a faceless voice said, "We will take the little girls—bring them to us, please."

The billeting officer pushed us up the front step, muttering, "They're sisters. They'll tell you their names."

And she disappeared into the dark.

CHAPTER 5

THE VERY REVEREND

"Come in, come in, my dears." The voice was gentle. "I'm Mrs. Bosworth. How nice for us to have you in our home."

Mrs. Bosworth looked like a picture in one of my fairy-tale books. Her hair was silvery, and her face was wrinkly, and she reminded me of my great-aunt Esther.

"Reverend Bosworth would be here to welcome you, but his rheumatism is bothering him. You'll meet him in a wee while."

Our rabbi at home was sometimes called Reverend Hyman, and I wondered whether Reverend Bosworth was a rabbi too. My knees felt wobbly and my heart thumped loudly. My feet seemed glued to the spot where that lady had pushed us. I clutched Viv's hand. She squeezed mine back and then pulled hard. I fell forward, smothering my face in Mrs. Bosworth's blue skirt. I was glad my face was hidden because I was trying to lick the salty tears that had reached my top lip, but Viv had already seen them.

"Stop it, cry-baby," she hissed. "Remember you promised to be brave."

She didn't need to remind me. I knew I had, but I wanted to stay wrapped in that soft, comfy skirt.

"Dear little ones, you must be so very tired. I'd like you to meet the Vicar, and then how about a bowl of bread and milk before I tuck you up in bed?"

I wondered how she knew that bread and milk was my most favourite food and that I always felt comforted after spoonfuls of hot, soggy bread and brown sugar. Would she put raisins in it like Mum did? And would they be all plumped up? At the thought of Mum, my tears rolled once more. Viv knew. She squeezed my hand again and said in her bossiest voice, "Please would you put raisins in if you have them, because that's the way Joy likes her bread and milk."

Mrs. Bosworth didn't seem to notice Viv's bossiness. "Certainly, I'll—"

But before she finished what she was going to say the front door slammed with a bang and we all jumped. A deep voice spoke from somewhere. "I was beginning to wonder when you were going to bring the little gals into the parlour. They must be freezing. That north wind was blowing right into my face."

I peered out from Mrs. Bosworth's sheltering skirt, and she put her arms around us both, and we all moved into the parlour. We didn't have a parlour in our London flat. We had our Everything Room. I was curious. What did a parlour look like? And who was the Vicar?

I had never met a vicar before. And was he the same person as the reverend?

But I needn't have been scared. Not of Reverend Bosworth. The colour of his hair resembled that of the pewter mug my grandpa received when he retired. His pink cheeks and wide smile of welcome gave me a warm feeling inside. He said we could call Mrs. Bosworth "Aunty Violet" and we could call him "Uncle Vicar," and he would explain later what a vicar was. Uncle Vicar was sitting in a chair that looked exactly the same as my grandpa Henry's favourite chair. Grandpa Henry called his chair "my wing-backed beauty."

I was glad to see Uncle Vicar's chair.

"I'm going to put the milk on now and leave you three to have a little talk—get to know each other. You'll have more time tomorrow, so you don't have to say everything now," Aunty Violet called as she disappeared through the door that led out of the parlour.

I didn't want her to vanish like that and started to follow her, but I looked up at Viv and knew by the way she was squeezing her lips that she wasn't going to say anything. She wasn't going to get to know Uncle Vicar, not right then, anyway.

I stayed beside her because the previous night Mum and Dad had said, "Be good girls," and I didn't want Uncle Vicar to think we didn't know our manners.

Dad had chuckled. "Remember, your father's a lady and your mother's a gentleman."

We screeched "Daaad" in chorus, but we didn't laugh. We usually did at that old joke, but not that night. It just didn't work. We were pretending that everything was the same as any other night.

But it wasn't.

We were acting then, and I wondered if I would be able to act now.

"Uncle Vicar"—it came out in a whisper—"do you have any girls or boys of your own?" I felt hot and my cheeks burned. The boys and girls in my class at Salisbury Road School called me "The Big Blusher."

That was a nosey thing to say, so I added quickly, "I mean, I mean er ..."

"No. Mother and I haven't any children of our own, but you know, you girls can be our family now."

"We have our own mother and father," Viv said breathily, her lower lip quivering.

"Of course you have, my dears, but you won't be ours for long, y'know. There's not going to be anything to worry about. All this trouble will be finished quite soon. Now let's go and see how Mother's getting on with that bread and milk."

It didn't seem easy for him to get out of his chair. I reached forward, put my hand on top of his, and pulled. I think I must have hurt him 'cos there were purply bruises on the back of his hands and big blue ridges that looked like railway lines crisscrossing in all directions.

"Thank you, my dear; you're a kind little girl."

My thumping heart sounded quieter, and suddenly I couldn't keep my eyes open a minute longer. I felt Viv's hand in the middle of my back, and her voice sounded as though it was in a long tunnel.

"She always does this. She can fall asleep anywhere—even standing up. I think I'd better help her into bed now. Would you be kind enough to show us where we are going to sleep?"

And then she started to cry.

My eyes popped open, and I joined her heaving wails.

Aunty Violet rushed out of the kitchen and bundled us up the staircase. I was fully awake now, and I couldn't stop wailing. The stairs were steep and I found it hard to lift my legs. I don't know how I did it, but I did. I was in a small bedroom; the wallpaper had tiny flowers dotted all over and there was a huge bed with a pale blue eiderdown on its top.

Aunty Violet lifted me up, and I plopped down in its middle. Uncle Vicar brought me my haversack, and Viv went downstairs to fetch hers.

"Now let's untie these labels. I think we know who you are, don't we?" He chuckled, but he couldn't undo the reef knot Dad had made, so he said, "Well, Mother, you're going to have to help me. My fingers are too bumbly."

I looked at the thin string on Viv's luggage label. It was white when we started, and now it was dirty. Her luggage label was creased and crumbled, and her name, Iris-Vivienne Abrahams, was streaky. I expect her tears had made the ink run, so I looked down at my label.

My name, Joy Ruth Abrahams, was smudged so badly I couldn't read it. Not one of my names. When I saw the burlap haversacks Mum had sewn on the Singer treadle the night before, I nearly started crying again but bit my top lip hard. I didn't want Viv to be cross. I expected she was worried like me, but she rarely showed it. Dad had called her hard. I thought that was a cruel thing to say.

Aunty Violet took my nightie from my haversack, held it up, and smoothed it gently. "My oh my, What a pretty nightie. Look, my dear, it matches the eiderdown. Pale-blue forget-me-nots on a pale-blue bed."

And before I could say "Jack Robinson," she had undressed me and popped my nightie over my head.

"We'll worry about a strip-wash tomorrow. I can see your big sister has found her nightie and is ready for bed."

I knew why Viv had undressed so quickly. She was eleven and had already told me she was growing up and that it wasn't right for anyone to see her without her clothes on.

Aunty Violet must have known because she said Uncle Vicar had gone downstairs to bring up our bread and milk. "When you've supped it all, you'll brush your teeth and say your prayers."

And that was the beginning of our first night. The bread and milk was scrumptious—even creamier than we had at home. Aunty Violet said that was because the milk came from the farmer down the lane who had a Jersey cow.

Uncle Vicar wanted to hear us say our prayers. He said he liked the way we said our special prayer, the *Shema*, and that he hadn't heard Hebrew spoken so nicely since he was at Divinity School, "and that was a long time ago."

They gave us a kiss and switched off the light and it was all dark. Pitch-black dark.

"Viv. Are you awake?"

"Of course I am."

"Sis."

"What?"

"I can't sleep in this bed."

"You can, stupid. Shut your eyes."

"Sing to me, sis. Please, let's sing. Sing 'Phil the Fluter's Ball.' Or let's recite 'Daffodils I wandered lonely as a cl—'"

"Oh stop it, Fatty. I'm tired too you know. I've looked after you all day, and I have to sleep right now." She turned over, moved to the edge of the bed, and wouldn't let me snuggle near her.

"Sis. Cuddle me. Please cuddle me."

She didn't answer, and I was frightened that she had gone to sleep before me. When she did that, I could never sleep. I was like that at home, even when we stayed at Grandma's with Mum and Dad. If I was the last one to go to sleep I was frightened. But now she had.

And I was alone. And awake. And scared.

I jumped. A soft hand stroked the side of my face, and I heard Aunty Violet whisper, "If you like, I'll lay beside you, little one, until you fall asleep."

As soon as she said that I felt my whole body change—all the air swooshed out of me like a balloon bursting. I must have fallen asleep right then because suddenly I was awake and I was alone in the big bed. The sun was streaming through the window, and Viv's head appeared around the door.

"Come on, sleepyhead, rise and shine. Porridge is on the table."

Everything was sunny in the kitchen, and there were flowers all over. Flowers on the curtains—yellow daisies; flowers on the table-cloth—pillar-box-red poppies; and flowers on Aunty Violet's pinafore—deep bronzy antirrhinums. All the flowers made me feel happy even though I wasn't quite sure if I ought to be. We sat in the breakfast nook to have our porridge and toast with thick raspberry jam. Almost the yummiest jam I'd ever tasted.

"It comes from the raspberry canes at the bottom of the garden. Uncle Vicar is out there now. He likes to potter in his greenhouse before he has his breakfast. You can join him when you're finished. I know he'd love to show you his prize tomatoes."

And that became our timetable—our daily routine. Each night Aunty Violet lay down beside me until I fell asleep. Each morning we had our breakfast in the breakfast nook, and then we joined Uncle Vicar in his greenhouse while Aunty Violet tidied the house. Uncle Vicar would pluck a plump, ripe tomato from his favourite vine, put it under his nose, close his eyes, and slowly sniff.

"Aaah," he would say breathily. "Smell this, little ones—the aroma of Eden."

We copied him. We closed our eyes, sniffed slowly, and breathed our aahs. I imagined I was in the Garden of Eden dancing with flowers in my hair and a daisy-chain around my neck. I did a little hop and skip and almost knocked a vine over, but Uncle Vicar steadied it.

He winked at me and in a twinkly voice, murmured, "Garden of Eden would be fun, wouldn't it, my dear?"

Aunty Violet and Uncle Vicar were kind to us every day and in every way, and I liked it when they hugged us. Viv was a bit stand-offish and was cross with me when I told her to let them hug her, but I could see she liked it too.

But all the trouble Uncle Vicar had said would soon be over wasn't. On our first Sunday in their home, the third of September 1939, Prime Minister Chamberlain announced that Britain and Germany were at war. We were gathered around the wireless while we heard his speech. The four of us sighed. Long, deep sighs. I'd learned about wars at school, but I'd never been in a war before and wondered if we'd all be killed. And would Viv and I die alone without Mum and Dad? If we were going to have to die, I wanted to die with them.

We heard Chamberlain say, "It is evil things we are fighting against … I am certain that right will prevail." Even though the news about the war beginning sounded bad, his words made us feel a little better. We all sat in silence but felt very close to each other and all of England.

I thought the whole world would be better if they were more like my uncle Eliezer, who didn't believe in wars. He called himself a pacifist. He and my uncle Barney used to argue a lot, and Uncle Barney always ended up shouting at Uncle Eliezer.

I remembered one particular argument: "You've buried your head in the sand, my dear brother-in-law. It's 1938 and you can't accept what's happening to us in Germany. It's been going on since 1933 when that paper-hanger, Hitler, came to power. They're killing us Jews. They want to get rid of us. And all because we're Jewish."

Uncle Barney would then go on about the different places that some Jews had managed to escape to, like Spain and France and Holland and even as far away as Argentina and China.

Dad said, "Why on earth would they go to Spain? Isabella and Ferdinand forced us to leave there in the 1500s. In 1492, to be exact. That's where our family originally came from; they fled to Holland and then came to England. We've been here for ages. I think it's the fault of the Enlightenment."

I didn't know what the Enlightenment was but didn't want to interrupt.

I heard Uncle Barney shout, "It's 1938, Eliezer. What about Kristallnacht? You want that to happen here?"

I worried that the hatred of Jews and talk of war might spread to England.

Uncle Eliezer said, "Now we're scaring the girls. Look at their faces."

I rubbed my pale cheeks with my fist.

Viv spoke up. "I read about Kristallnacht in the paper. And before that they had huge bonfires where they burned books."

"Some Jewish people had the good sense to get out early," said Dad. "I read that in 1933 there were already more than thirty thousand interned in concentration camps. I'm glad the Felds got out in '38. Did you ever hear their stories, Eli?"

I knew Mr. and Mrs. Feld. They played bridge with Mum and Dad. Mr. Feld had been a famous artist in Germany. He used to tell us about his favourite paintings—where you could see them, and what school they belonged to. He made us feel grown up, and I liked him. He didn't laugh when I said I didn't know that painters had to belong to a school. He explained it. I didn't always understand what he meant, but Viv did and she would go over it again with me later. He said Viv had all the makings of an artist because she had a good eye and was sensitive. I was kind of jealous, but not too much.

I was glad my family was aware of right and wrong, but I didn't know how to tell Aunty Violet and Uncle Vicar about my uncle Eliezer. Viv told me everyone hated pacifists. She said that if you were British you had to be patriotic and that if you weren't, it was treason. You could be hung for treason. The only man accused of treason that I knew about was Guy Fawkes. He tried to blow up the Houses of Parliament. I felt sure I could ask Uncle Vicar about the Enlightenment, treason, and being a pacifist and patriotic at the same time. I thought I'd wait a few days.

Six days and nights went by in a flash, and I forgot to ask Uncle Vicar those questions. Our days were busy. We helped dust and mop. We helped pick raspberries, blackberries, and loganberries. And we tried to help Uncle Vicar with the *Times* crossword puzzle. We were good at dusting and mopping, and at picking, but we weren't good at crosswords. Uncle Vicar said the *Times*' clues were very literary, and that when we were older we'd solve them in two shakes of a lamb's tail. Uncle Vicar made me laugh a lot; so did Aunty Violet. She taught us about word puns. She told me that I latched onto the idea of puns like a mischievous sprite. She quoted William Shakespeare: "Hast thou yet latched the Athenian's eyes with the love juice?" Viv had been in *A Midsummer Night's Dream* and had played Puck. I liked the thought of love juice and that line had stuck in my mind when Viv said it.

I told Aunty Violet that Viv had acted well and we were all proud of her.

Then she told us her secret. When she was seventeen the Royal Academy of Dramatic Art had offered her a place, but her father was against it because he didn't approve of the acting life, so she became a teacher. Aunty Violet said that's when she learned the value of patience. I knew she was patient. She never seemed to mind that I couldn't crack eggs without getting the bits of eggshell in the yolks. Aunty Violet and Uncle Vicar were gentle and kind and made us feel comfortable, even though we missed Mum and Dad every day.

The government had shut all the schools for a week, so Aunty Violet said we could go and play on the swings in the school playground. We did.

Each day, after tea, we pumped ourselves on the swings. High, high in the sky. We escaped into the white clouds and blue sky and sang, "Pack up your troubles in your old kit-bag and smile, smile, smile."

CHAPTER 6
EYEING THE BUCKLE

We were hot, dusty, and tired. We saw the front door open. We saw the lady from across the street standing in the doorway. We saw our haversacks in the hallway. I felt an enormous stone in my throat. It wouldn't let me speak. Not one word. I clutched Viv's hand and looked at her face. She was sheet-white, and her eyes didn't stop blinking. We didn't know what or why, but we knew.

The lady spoke in a funny way. "You're both coming to stay at my house. The dear Reverend has had a stroke, and Mrs. Bosworth will have her hands full looking after him without having you two as well. She's with him at the Cottage Hospital now, but the Reverend has to stay a few days until they know if he's out of the woods. Anyway, they can't keep you, so you have to move. Pick up your things right now."

Whoever had packed our haversacks had stuffed our clothes in willy-nilly and the sack wouldn't sit straight or fit properly on my back. I took the straps and pulled mine across the road. Viv did the same.

"You pick those sacks up and wear them properly. If you're going to stay with me you have to do what I say and when I say it. Mr.

Short expects obedience too. When he tells you to do something, you'd better do it. That's the way we've brought up our own five, and we're not going to do anything different now. I'm certainly not going to spoil you like Mrs. Bosworth did. I've got my hands full enough without two spoilt Jews."

It was our seventh day away from home as we dragged our feet to the Shorts' house. We were moving to our second billet. They seemed the opposite of the Bosworths. I never imagined that being evacuated was going to be like this.

The houses across from Uncle Vicar's house were all joined together. They were called terrace houses. They were dark and gloomy. Their bricks were a dirty grey colour, and their doorknockers and door handles were dull and almost brown, not shiny and golden like Aunty Violet's. Between every two houses was an arch-shaped tunnel that looked eerie. Mrs. Short led us into the tunnel. It smelled of cat pee and dirt. At the end there were two iron gates.

"Our gate is this side."

The latch squealed as she lifted it.

"Don't you ever go in that side," she threatened, "If you do, their bulldog'll bite you.

"Our lav is down there, see, at the bottom of the garden."

Where she pointed seemed miles away and I knew I wouldn't be able to go there alone once it was dark. I'd been in the outdoor lav at the cricket grounds and had to hold my nose every time.

"This is the back door," she continued. "*Never* go in the front door. We unlock it on Sundays when we go to church but on no other days. And you'll have to come with us. I'm not leaving you two alone in our home. Who knows what you might get up to?"

Viv and I hadn't said a word so far. Mrs. Short had done all the talking, and I hated every word I heard. I was sure Viv did too. But before we could whisper to each other, she had pushed us into a small scullery where a copper boiler was chugging.

Five people crowded in; they stared at us curiously. The three girls looked like grownup ladies to me with their bright red lipstick and red rouged cheeks and blonde hair curled in pageboys.

They didn't smile.

The tallest one said, "Now where are they going to sleep, Mother? I'm not sharing my room with anyone."

"Mind your manners. Be a Christian and say hello," said Mrs. Short. "I'm doing the Reverend a favour. Anyway, it won't be for long—I'll be calling the billeting officer in the morning."

"Mum." The fatter boy laughed. "They look so puny."

The other boy sniggered, stuck his tongue out, put his thumb to his nose, waggled his fingers, and rolled his eyeballs up until only the whites showed.

I moved as close as I could to Viv and squeezed her hand hard.

"They must be dumb. Can't they speak? P'raps they don't know their own names," the boys screeched. "Me! I ain't sharing my room with them. Put them in the box-room, Mum."

"Yes, Mother," the tall girl said. "I'll clear out those old clothes. Last time I was in there it stunk. I found a dead mouse in the trap. A stinking corpse."

The meanest boy jumped up and down, pointing his finger. He laughed, "Corpsey Corpsey's come to greet the Cockneys."

Viv spoke in her poshest voice. "We are not Cockneys. We were not born within the sound of Bow Bells."

I wished I had said that.

A very loud voice yelled, "Well bring those Cockneys in. Let's have a look at them."

"Now move, you lot," and Mrs. Short led us into the kitchen. "Here they are, and goodness knows how we're going to manage to eat. There's hardly any room as it is round the table. We'll have to fetch those old stools that are in the shed. You boys go brush the cobwebs off. Go on. Father, did you hear what Allie said? There's a dead'un in the box-room. That's where they're going to have to sleep, so send Tabby up there; she's a good mouser. I'm surprised she wasn't scratching the door."

Mr. Short sat at the table and stared at us. His trousers had black grease stains in blobs and patches that looked like a Morse code message. The sleeves of his dark-blue work shirt were torn, and his wide brown leather belt had a huge buckle on the end.

"I see you're eyeing my belt. Don't think you can get away with nothing here. All mine have felt this belt on their bums, and yours will feel it too if you're lippy."

"Now Father, don't scare them or they'll have nightmares and our sleep'll be done for."

"Come on, you girls get the supper on the table. We'll eat, you lot will clean up the kitchen, and I'll clear out the box-room and get these two into bed."

"I'm not hungry." Nothing could have gone past that stone in my throat.

"Nor am I." Viv put her arm around me and pulled me close.

"None of that here now. You'll eat what's set before you, and you'll sit there until it's all finished, d'ya hear?"

I felt Viv's whole body tighten.

"And don't make no faces at me 'cos it ain't going to help you none."

I wished I could have been inside Viv's skin.

"Here, you two, sit on this settee. I'll make you some jam sandwiches. That'll probably be enough for you tonight." Mrs. Short's voice sounded kinder than before and she half-smiled. We sat down and waited.

Mr. Short was still looking at us, and he burst into laughter. A laugh that made his whole body shake. "Now don't you two look so scared. My kids say my bark is worse than my bite. If you do as you're told, everything will be all right. Ya can do that, can't ya?"

"Yes, sir," we said eagerly.

"And I don't need no sirring. Call me Pap like the others do."

"Yes, Pap. Yes."

Suddenly all the Shorts were laughing and talking at once and hurrying around the kitchen and scullery; it felt like a gust of wind had blown through the back door and carried the scares away. The boys made faces at us, but now they were funny faces, not mean ones. The jam in our sandwiches oozed from the sides and the bread was about an inch thick (doorstops we called them), but we ate them 'cos we were hungry and I wasn't choked up any longer. Viv licked the jam off her fingers and I copied her. I felt babyish sucking my fingers, but no one noticed. The tabby cat jumped up onto my lap and started playing the piano on my thighs, her sharp claws marking time. It hurt but I didn't say a word.

Pap grinned as he said, "That's a good sign. Our Tabby seems to like you. She doesn't play the piano on them that don't smell right. P'raps you little uns'll fit in after all." He became sharp again. "Now, Mother, turn the wireless on. You know I can't miss the news. Gotta keep up with what's going on in this bloody war. Now turn that volume up and shut up all you kids. You know the rule. No talking when the news is on."

The scream of a siren filled the air, its wail rising and falling repeatedly. It sounded ominous and was followed by the announcer's serious voice.

"You have just heard an air-raid siren. When you hear the sound of the siren go to your air-raid shelter immediately. When you hear this different tone"—a long, even note was played—"it's the all–clear, and you can return to your home."

We heard the yells of the boys above the all-clear. They had been sitting cross-legged, side-by-side in front of Pap and had snorted at the siren's sounds. Pap had boxed their ears, one ear with his right fist, the other with his left.

"It ain't funny. Shut your mouths. Listen. The whole family could be killed in an air raid. War ain't no game."

I was all mixed up. We were going to sleep in a box-room where a mouse had died. We didn't know if the Shorts had a bed for us or a place to put our things. We didn't know if Pap would hit us if we spoke when we weren't supposed to. The only thing we did know was that the Shorts didn't really want to have us.

"Upstairs, you two. Say g'night to Pap and everyone."

"Viv," I whispered, "I can't remember their names." Viv's memory was perfect. We called her our "Family Memory Bank."

"Good night, Pap; good night, Mother Short; good night, Alice and Edna and Kate. Good night James and Ernest."

They roared with laughter as she recited the list.

"You can call them Allie, Edie, Kitty, Jimmy, and Ernie. We ain't high falutin' here. And you can call me Ma Short."

I rehearsed those names inside my head and hoped I would remember them in the morning.

We followed Ma Short to a door in the wall of the kitchen. She opened it. Inside were wooden steps that went up forever. We clumped up after her. There were five doors off the landing at the top. She opened the one that was narrower and lower than the rest.

"This is where you're going to have to kip down. Don't you go into the other rooms; they're ours. I suppose I'll have to give you a chamber pot. I don't want you making a noise when you go out to the privy. You can leave the lamp on. I'll turn it off when I come to bed."

We peeked into the room.

"Oh good! I see Allie has found a potty and some blankets. Get in there and get off to sleep and don't get up too early. G'night."

She pushed us in, pulled the door shut, and clumped down the stairs, the echo of her hard heels coinciding with the twitch in Viv's eyes. The oil lamp sat on a small stool in one corner. Our haversacks were in the other, and the mattress took up the rest of the space.

"It's a straw mattress, Joy. Like the one we slept on when we went to Somerset with Mum and Dad and slept in Farmer Gee's barn." We'd enjoyed ourselves on his farm. "That's why it smells funny in here," she said seriously, as we fell onto it.

I thought she was saying that to help me forget about the fusty smell and the mice that might have died there.

"Let's pretend we've discovered a secret place. And we're going to shrink to fit inside."

I knew she was trying to make me feel better, help me take my mind off being sad. It worked.

"It's a bit like Alice's hole, isn't it?" I giggled.

"If Pap Short was smaller, he could be the Mad Hatter."

Viv snorted. "We can have a tea party. We'll make the fairy cakes like Aunty Violet showed us."

It was hard not to feel sad again when I heard Aunty Violet's name, but a scritchle-scratchle at the door interrupted that feeling. It was followed by a soft, "Meow. Meow."

"Tabby's come to join the tea party." Viv laughed, and let him in. He sniffed around and then jumped right onto the pillows at the top of the mattresses. It looked as though he was smiling, and I thought of the Cheshire Cat.

We found our nighties, undressed quickly, and got under the covers. Tabby squeezed in between us. "Purr. Purr. Puuurrrr."

The sounds were comforting. The straw mattress was prickly, but we wriggled our bodies around to form a hollow that fit our shapes.

We began our ritual: we said the *Shema*, we held hands, and we softly sang our songs: "Harbour Lights." "Red Sails in the Sunset." "Poor Butterfly." I closed my eyes. Our ritual worked! The next thing I heard was Tabby's scratching at the door.

"Let her out, Viv. She's like me; she probably wants to go to the bathroom."

Then I remembered. "I'll have to put my coat on to go down the garden. Come with me, Viv. Please. Please."

Viv promised she would come this time but that I was going to have to get used to going to the privy by myself.

"Anyway, Ma Short said she was going to call the billeting officer this morning. We may not be staying here too long."

The thought of being somewhere else again made me shudder.

Our Mum often said, "Better the devil you do know than the devil you don't." I quoted that to Viv, but she added, "You never know. It's possible that there are more people in the village like Uncle Vicar and Aunty Violet but not as old. They might even have a car and a nice house."

I didn't want those things. I wanted someone who was kind and would like me. But most of all I wanted to go home.

"Up. Up. All of you," a hoarse voice barked outside our door. We were dressed and downstairs with Tabby before the loud clobber of the other children's feet followed.

"Quick. Down the garden before the others hog the privy. There's always a queue after Pap gives his get-up order. You'll get used to it if you're staying. But you're making us cramped, y'know, and the five bob Ma will get for each of you won't stretch no further than a broke elastic band."

They kept on rubbing it in. All the time. All of them. How "those bloody evacuees are a thievin' lot, nicking us blind. How they smell, how they eat, how they speak." Nothing any Londoner did was right.

So I was surprised when one night at teatime Ma Short shouted at her family, "That's enough you lot. Londoners've got their ways and we've got ours. Yeh, they're different but they're humans like us. God brought them here on earth."

"Ah I dunno about that, Ma," said Pap. "Not with these two. I ain't sure Jews believe in God."

I choked on my biscuit. Viv thought for a minute and defiantly stood up and recited the poem we hadn't dared to recite in September: "How odd of God to choose the Jews. But not so odd as those who choose a Jewish God yet spurn the Jews."

At first the Shorts looked stunned, but after a minute or two, when the words had sunk in, Pap chortled. "That's a good 'un. Who taught you that?"

"My dad did," boasted Viv.

Ma Short drew in a breath of dismay. "Oh, I forgot. I was supposed to give you this. The billeting office brought a letter from your parents." She pulled an envelope from her purse. "They hadn't been told where you had been billeted since Reverend Bosworth's illness. They were worried. They asked me to tell you that they are coming to see you. On Sunday."

It was only Monday. We thought, will Sunday ever come?

It did come and there they were, our own parents. Our own mum and dad. They walked toward us down that long, long street. The six-week separation had felt like ten thousand. We pulled at the buckles of our roller skates, breaking the worn leather, and stumbled and ran and fell into Mum's arms. I buried my head in her soft big belly, unable to speak. I was crying and was hot and cold at the same time. My lips were clenched; not a word came out, but inside I was screaming, *Mum! Mum! Mum!*

The pain of the separation started to dissolve. My sister too was burying her head in Mum's warm and generous belly, hugging and hugging. We lifted our heads at the same time and stood back to revel in her presence. Not a word was spoken. Silence. We beamed from ear to ear.

"How about a kiss for your dad?" Our tall father was standing back. His face looked as though it was trying to smile.

We rushed to him, smothering him with kisses. We had left him out. We swarmed over him, chattering excitedly. But I saw his face. I felt his hurt.

"Could we meet Mr. and Mrs. Short? We wondered if they would like to try the challah we bought from Monikendams." Dad took the bread out of his carrier bag.

Its familiar smell was heavenly.

Monikendams was a place that made your mouth water even if you had only one foot inside the entrance. It was filled with enticing pastries and breads. We always bought our Sabbath bread there. We hadn't spent our Friday nights welcoming the Sabbath since we'd been at the Shorts, and I wasn't sure whether Dad and Mum knew.

I couldn't understand why Ma Short was so unfriendly to our parents. Perhaps it was because we knocked at the front door and didn't go round the back, but when she opened the front door she didn't invite us in. She came outside in her thick winter coat and a round pot-shaped hat on her head.

"We have to go out now to help my cousin move. We'll be back at six, so you two can spend the day with your parents." She nodded to Mum. "Nice to meet you. Good-bye."

Mum and Dad were speechless. We turned and went down the street, and when we were out of sight we started laughing. Just like old times. In Dad's carrier bag, along with the challah, were apples and *vorst* sandwiches and Mum's poppy seed twist and a thermos full of jasmine tea.

The tea was piping hot. We liked our liquids hot. We found the park and sat on benches, had our picnic, and watched some little kids on the swings.

As the time drew near for their bus to leave, our talking stopped.

We leaned close together. We held the moments in our hearts.

CHAPTER 7
THE BOURNES

A few days after Mum and Dad had returned to London, we were in for another surprise. We had left school, running all the way so we wouldn't be late and make Ma Short cross, and there were our haversacks on the doorstep sitting lopsided.

Ma Short was at the door with her laundry basket on her hip. Abruptly and grumpily she said, "Good-bye, then."

We didn't know why we were being moved. Our frightened expressions must have softened her, because she added, "Look. We can't keep you any longer. We've had you for six weeks and we only took you in because the Rev had had a stroke. Anyway, you're too much for me. We're all on top of each other. Those weekly baths and all that washing'll be the death of me. I didn't expect the war to be this long—nearly two months—they're going to have to find someone else who'll foster you."

The billeting officer had appeared behind us and spoke briskly. "Girls, thank Mrs. Short for having you. Pick up your sacks and let's get going. Hurry! I have to get home to feed my own family after this move."

Viv was helping me balance my haversack on my back when Jimmy ran out holding a large carrier bag. "You've forgotten these things," he said as he punched my arm hard like he always did when he returned home from school.

Viv and I had no brothers of our own, and we hadn't known much about boys when we came to the Shorts'. Jimmy was thirteen and had teased us a lot the first fortnight. He had made fun of the way we spoke, flicked our gym-slips up with pencils so he could see our knickers, pinched me when Pap Short wasn't looking, and laughed when I cried. He didn't do that to Viv because she pinched him right back. Edie and Kitty stood up for us sometimes, but I expect they were happy they were no longer pinched. I liked Ernie better. He told me jokes when Jimmy was playing outside.

But now I didn't know what to think, except that once more everything was happening too fast. The bruises on my arms would have a chance to fade, but where were we going and who was going to look after us?

Tears, never far away, filled my eyes, but they made Viv cross. "Don't start crying again," she hissed as she jerked her head at the billeting officer. "She's probably found us another billet."

I took the carrier bag from Jimmy and made sure my books and special hankies—Mum's lace and Dad's spotted ones—were there, the ones I put on my pillow-slip every night to remember them.

Before we could follow the officer, Ma Short came running out. "Wait! Wait! My friend will take them. She's our church organist. Her daughter is the same age as that one. They'll probably play together without fighting." Under her breath she added, "The Bournes have spoilt their little precious. I think she's a bit of a handful!"

"I expect that will be okay," said the billeting officer. "We're short of homes to foster these kids. It's a big mess at the office. Here's the name of the chief lady there. The Bournes will need to go down and sign the papers to get the money for the kids." Without a wave, she left us.

Ma Short said coolly, "You can give the name of the chief lady to Mrs. Bourne. She'll find out where the office is."

Viv and I nudged each other. Viv asked, "Are we were to be *born again* like new babes in an old litter?"

The Bournes house was nearby. We walked with Ma Short down one street, turned left, and walked one street over. I wanted to run to Aunty Violet's, but I knew I wouldn't find my way back. We both shuffled. And counted. The Bournes would be our third billet.

In the past, three had been my lucky number. Would it be lucky this time?

As she opened a newly painted gate and pushed us in, Ma Short said quickly, "Good-bye, you two."

We walked up the path with our heads down as our eyes felt unwilling to see what might be in front of us.

"Put your heads up. Let's see what you look like," a voice shouted from the open doorway. A tall man dressed in army clothes was holding a girl close to him. We saw her rosy cheeks and long fair hair curled in ringlets. She peered at us from behind spectacles that magnified her eyes.

"I don't think she can see us," Viv whispered.

I didn't think so either, and I reminded Viv about our great-uncle Harry's eyesight. He could hardly see in front of his nose, and the glass in his frames was as thick as a welder's mask.

Behind the man and the girl stood a woman who towered over them both. She also wore spectacles that magnified her eyes, and her voice was loud. She boomed, "We're fostering you. For how long, that depends on you. You will obey my niece without fail. My brother will be away with his army corps, and my sister is the organist at our church. She may need one of you to help her blow the bellows on the organ, whichever of you is stronger."

She looked us over, seeming to judge our strength. Viv took my hand and squeezed it. Her squeeze was strong. Perhaps she wanted to help blow the bellows.

Will I have to blow them like I blow a balloon? I wondered.

The tall lady interrupted my thoughts. "We are the Bournes. I am Miss Bourne, my brother is Mr. Bourne, his wife is Mrs. Bourne, and their daughter is Helen. Do not shorten our names. Your names are …?" She waited for our replies.

Viv gulped and said, "Viv."

I quickly squeaked, "Joy."

"I said no shortening of names. What is your full name?" She pointed at Viv.

"Viv," Viv lied.

"Joyce," I lied, copying my clever sister.

Miss Bourne exploded. "Give me your full names immediately!"

"Vivienne-Iris Abrahams," my sister said, looking troubled.

"Joyce Ruth Abrahams," I continued lying. I had never liked the name Joyce, and perhaps if the Bournes called me by that name, the real me wouldn't be in this billet.

Helen Bourne was the family's prized possession. She was bossy and mean and cruel, especially when she called us Stinky and Smelly. Viv and I called her Hellybelly.

We thought Miss Bourne babied her. She would warm the rim of a flowery chamber pot with hot water for Hellybelly to "tinkle." We laughed at the word tinkle. We had never heard it used in that way before. We didn't "tinkle," we "peed," and we had to sit on a cold seat. We were not allowed to use Helen's potty and had to use the only lavatory in the house, which was upstairs where the Bournes lived.

We slept and played in a large, chilly storage room downstairs. The family would allow us to eat three meals a day with them at their dining room table. We were often still hungry, because at every meal, the Bournes' plates had more food on them than ours. We wondered whether Mr. Bourne had extra meat, butter, and sugar food coupons because he was in the army.

"Soldiers need full stomachs," his sister said primly. "It keeps them warm."

Mr. Bourne proclaimed, "No shortage of food yet, but I expect there'll be a tightening of our food coupon allowance soon."

Later that night in the basement, I said to Viv, "It wouldn't surprise me if they were in the black market."

"They are snobby. Have you heard the way they speak to their cleaning lady?" she replied.

We hated it there. We were living in two worlds: upstairs, where the temperature was always warm, and downstairs, where Viv and I were cold day and night. Neither of us had to blow the bellows for Mrs. Bourne, so we blew on each other, trying to make our breaths hot enough to warm our bodies.

Every day we had to take Hellybelly to school. Mrs. Bourne was busy practicing the organ for church, and Miss Bourne was doing housework. We had to make sure Hellybelly had the right books for the day. The boys and girls in her class made fun of her, and Viv and I tried to protect her from the mean things they said. We knew what it was like to be made fun of. This was made particularly difficult because Hellybelly was such a name-caller herself.

She wanted us to play games with her after school. We told her we wouldn't play if she continued being nasty when her parents weren't there.

"I wonder if she'll change," Viv said to me.

I wondered if people could ever change.

CHAPTER 8

SCARLET FEVER

I woke one night burning hot, feeling as though I was on fire. I sat up, looked around, but could see no flames. My arms, chest, and face were boiling. A red-hot poker was burning my throat; my stomach hurt, and I tried not to vomit.

Why hadn't my fiery limbs woken Viv? "Wake up, sis! Wake up! I'm on fire!"

"No you're not! *Oy vey.* Yes you are," she said, touching my cheeks and my forehead.

Mrs. Bourne came downstairs. "It's nearly two in the morning," she said sharply. "Quiet you two." She drew in a breath. "Goodness, you're as red as a pillar-box and your body's on fire. Mr. Bourne, Mr. Bourne!" she called, "I think this kid's got scarlet fever! We're going to have to send her to the Fever Hospital. She can't stay here and infect our Helen. It's a dangerous disease, and you can be left with troubled kidneys and a funny heart. I ought never to have offered to take in Jews. I expect those kids' clothes are full of diseases. I'm going to call an ambulance, and they'll deal with her."

She turned to us and glared. "I hope for your sakes you didn't infect our Helen. I don't want to sue your parents for damages."

The Bournes packed our possessions into our haversacks, and we waited and waited. Finally the Fever ambulance arrived, and two white-coated attendants loaded us in.

On the way, Viv told me her own heart had sunk when she heard they would send me to the Fever Hospital. "What will Mum do? Will she know where you are? She doesn't know the Bournes are our latest foster home. I'm not going to stay with them without you, Joy."

The ambulance ride was bumpy, churning my stomach. I couldn't stop vomiting, and the ambulance man in a white uniform cleaned me with wet cloths and bathed my forehead with damp towels. "Have to get your fever down before Matron sees it," he said as he shook a thermometer vigorously." It's still near 104 degrees. She'll probably be in solitary isolation for the first month," he said to Viv.

"Will they let me go with her?" Viv asked, her voice sounding querulous.

"No. You and your mum can only speak to your sister through a window. Matron's strict, one of the old-school—wimple neatly pressed, and uniform starched stiff as a board."

"Are we almost there?" I asked.

"Shut your eyes and sleep," he said. "It'll take another hour."

Later, when Viv and I discussed my time in hospital, she told me that she had *plotzed* when she heard the ambulance man say we would be separated.

I also learned later from Viv that when we arrived at the entrance to the hospital, there were two nurses with masks over their mouths who lifted me, sleeping and fevered, onto a stretcher, and I disappeared down a white-painted corridor.

The matron came from another ghostly corridor to talk with Viv, carrying a clipboard with sheets of paper. Viv hoped the papers showed the address of the hospital and how to contact Mum at our London address. Matron had a surprise for Viv in a small office. Mum was there.

Both she and Viv cried. Matron put her hands over her ears to deafen the sobs. "That's enough, Mrs. Abrahams. Here are the rules for the fever isolation unit:

- Parents are not allowed inside the unit. You may talk to your child through the window.
- Do not knock on the window with your hand or your umbrella if it is raining in the courtyard.
- The benches are for you to sit on. Do not lie on them.
- No children under eight years are allowed in the courtyard."

A nurse came into the office and said, "Come, I'll show you the way."

Sighing with relief, Mum and Viv followed the nurse into the courtyard. There were windows around three sides. They could see nothing behind them. The glass panes were blank.

Anxiously, Viv asked, "Mum, where is Joy? Where has Matron put her?"

Luckily Matron appeared inside behind a window and pointed to a cot that was covered with a huge muslin net. Viv and Mum looked through but were unable to see me. I looked like an envelope wrapped in white sheets. A white-coated nurse helped me to turn my head and look through the window. They waved, greeting me with all the gestures of love that they knew: blowing kisses with their hands, squeezing their arms around themselves, jumping up and down with eyes and mouths wide open. I remembered lip reading to a friend of our grandma Hal who was deaf as we tried to lip read through the panes. Mum tried hard to make her conversation cheerful, opening her lips as wide as she could. Viv copied her. My head was wobbly. The nurse placed a mask over my mouth, making a shooing gesture to them. It was time for them to leave.

I was in the solitary isolation unit for one month. I felt very lonely and bored. My throat was sore all the time. The only thing that relieved it was when they gave me ice cubes. There were some children's books and comics to read, but they were tattered and torn and stories I'd read before. Time passed slowly, and I wished I could make it go faster but didn't know how.

I missed my family so much, especially my mum. Viv was still staying with the Bournes and attending school. Mum had to work back in London and look after Dad.

There was a girl three beds away from mine, and her mum was allowed to come visit inside the unit. I couldn't understand why one mother was allowed to visit her daughter and mine wasn't. It felt so unfair.

We celebrated the day that my fever broke and Matron told us I would no longer be isolated. Mum and Viv bought a cake with one candle and jumped excitedly outside my window. It would be another month before I would be discharged.

My family asked Matron worriedly, "Where shall the girls go? Who will take a foster child who has been in hospital with scarlet fever?"

Matron replied, "One of my nurses is fond of young Joy. She has neighbours, a kind, thoughtful couple who she is sure will help out. My nurse will ask them, and we'll give you their reply."

My bout with scarlet fever had taken its toll on Viv, on Mum, on Dad stuck in London, and on me.

When I was finally given the "all-clear," I had lost one stone (fourteen pounds) and was as thin as a pencil.

Mum said she had lost almost three-quarters of a stone. "All that asking for time off from work, rushing to catch the Green Line to the hospital, and worrying how you two were and how Dad was in London. I'll probably put that weight back on," she said wistfully.

We had missed Dad and hoped we could make up for lost time. We had hardly seen him. He'd been busy working as a mechanic, fixing motor engines for the war effort, and was not allowed time off.

Viv and I were closer than ever. We couldn't bear to be separated. She asked me to tell her what it felt like to be masked and bandaged in wet wrappings.

"Ugh!" I grimaced. "I want to forget the horrid things they did, not remember them. I'll tell you when we're both older and my memory has softened."

We counted the number of times they had been to visit me in the hospital. In the two months, Mum had been five times, and Viv was given permission by her teacher to be absent from school one day a week and visited me nine times. She hadn't much money, and her school gave her a bus ticket to cover the fare. A billeting officer had found a bed for her in a hostel for refugees, which was near our own home. They were grownup refugees and spoke languages she didn't understand. She did her homework and kept to herself. It was difficult to sleep. She said the inside of her head felt like a whizzing roundabout.

On our last day, Matron said the "nice couple" would have us in their home as foster children. "The billeting officer will be here soon and will drive you there."

We said our good-byes and thank yous. I was glad billeting officers were given extra gas coupons to schlep people like us from home to home.

CHAPTER 9
THE CANNS

Away we went with a tired billeting officer in a tired-looking, beat-up Morris. When we finally arrived, she parked the car and we followed her down the street. I couldn't lift my head.

I stared at the paving stones and saw patterns where the cracks joined. I couldn't keep up with either Viv or the billeting officer, who told us her name was Mrs. Thistlethwaite.

That stopped my welling tears, and I started to snicker until Viv gave me The Eye.

"It's not far," said Mrs. Thistlethwaite. "The Canns are in the next street."

I wanted to show off my punning skills and whispered, "What kind of can is this going to be?" I got another Eye from Viv.

On our street in London we played Kick the Can until the tips of our shoes were scarred.

"Are we going to be like sardines? Large can or small?" I got the Third Eye from Viv and a kick on the ankle—not too hard, but hard enough.

Mrs. Thistlethwaite was a fast walker. I had to trot to keep up, and my large burlap haversack thumped rhythmically and painfully against my bottom. I sat down on the pavement. I didn't want to go any further.

"It's not far; it's not far now." Mrs. Thistlethwaite's voice came in small, breathy jumps. "We're almost there."

And suddenly we were.

The huge house was squarish and stood by itself in the middle of a large garden. Everything about it appeared friendly. The garden was full of flowers: irises and antirrhinums, hollyhocks and calendulas; there were birch and oak trees, even a weeping willow, as well as a wide arch covered with honeysuckle. It was like a painting come to life.

"Pinch me," whispered Viv. "Tell me I'm not dreaming."

The front door opened, and out came a small, chubby man. He walked toward us, arms outstretched. His face was alive, his curved smile reached from ear to ear, and his eyes shined their welcome. Even his ears wriggled invitingly. "Greetings, greetings, greetings, little ones. I'm Mr. Cann. That's can with two ns."

He peered into my face in a knowing way, as if he knew all about my previous punning.

I grinned. I felt certain things were going to change.

His shaggy-haired sheepdog, all grey and white, bounded up energetically and licked our hands and legs. "Now then, Myrtle, cease that slobbering, I expect the girls have washed their hands for tea. Ma's been making ham sandwiches, trifle, and fairy cakes ever since Mrs. Thistlethwaite let her know these little 'uns were coming."

Dear God, I thought. Doesn't he know we don't eat ham? Hasn't anyone told him we're Jewish? We turned to look for Mrs. Thistlethwaite, but she had rushed off home.

My brave Viv spoke up. "Mr. Cann, my sister and I are Jewish, and we don't eat ham or pork or shellfish. I hope you don't mind."

"Mind, luv?" He beamed. "Of course I don't mind, and I know Ma will be delighted. There aren't any members of the Jewish faith in our village, and you can be our very first Jewish friends. Yes. Ma will be delighted."

He said it with such certainty it calmed me right down. He put his arms around us both as he propelled us gently into the house, saying, "Now, come and meet Ma."

Ma was in the kitchen, a warm, snug kitchen with pots, pans, and dishes set higgledy-piggledy in every nook and cranny, yet it wasn't messy. I didn't have time to work out how that could be because Ma brushed my cheek with her cool hand.

She said breathlessly, "Would you like us to show you around now, or shall we all have tea first?"

My cheek tickled and tingled and then Ma hugged Viv and me and it was almost as if our own dear Mum was there saying, "It's all right to let Ma do this—she's standing in for me."

Viv's tummy rumbled, and even Myrtle cocked her ears, and we pretended to copy her and tilted our heads to catch the rumbling.

Mr. Cann chortled. "Okay. Okay. Your tummies are telling us it's tea first. Now let's get this business of names over with. Ma's 'Ma,' I'm Uncle Cann, and you're …?" He looked at us inquiringly.

Viv blurted, "My name's Iris, but I like my middle name Viv better. I think I'll change it soon. My sister's name is Joy. You can call her Joy-Ruth, and she might even let you call her *Simcha*, which means 'Joy' in Hebrew."

At the sound of "Simcha," Myrtle jumped up and licked my face. I fell in love with her then and there.

Every morsel of our first tea melted in our mouths: the fairy cakes, the scones with raspberry jam, the sandwiches with the ham taken out, and the trifle with real Devonshire cream. Then came more magic. Uncle Cann led us into the garden.

"These are my aviaries, my little birds, my friends. Listen to their sweet singing, and find the colours of the rainbow."

The sound of birdsong filled our ears as we named the colours we knew—alizarin red, crimson, magenta, cerulean blue, turquoise, sea green.

The magic continued. I didn't have to imagine I was in Wonderland, because I was.

Viv agreed with me. The next morning we wrote our weekly letter to Mum and Dad, describing everything in detail.

A few days later as we walked to school, Viv told me, "Ma can't get warm enough and she asked me to sleep in her bed with her. So I did. You sleep like a log, Joy. You didn't even hear her come into our room last night, did you?"

That was true. Ma moved quietly even though she was plump like Mum. She had a fat tummy, curly brown hair, grey-blue eyes, pale cheeks, and a soft, soft voice.

"It's me, Myrtle, and our birds who make all the noise around here," Uncle Cann joked. "Ma's glad you've joined our family."

Ma showed her gladness in many ways. She had a hidden surprise waiting for us every single day when we returned from school. We had to find it. She called it "Ma's Scavenger Hunt" and wrote clever clues to help us, such as: "Find me. I'm close to being in my prime." Viv found that surprise. She knew all about prime numbers and said it was probably hidden near the front gate. She found the number 11 near the latch. Ma hid books, knitted gloves, brooches and hair slides, coloured ankle socks, and tiny jam tarts. She said we had to be quick with those clues, otherwise Myrtle would pip us to the post.

We loved Uncle Cann and Ma in the same way we had loved Aunty Violet and Uncle Vicar. It was how I imagined living in a fairyland would be.

Uncle Cann left for his work at the factory early. Every morning he carried cups of tea upstairs for Ma, Viv, and me without spilling a single drop in the saucers.

"Good morning. Good morning. Good morning, my family," he would call in one breath.

It was as though we were part of the card game Happy Families, where you tried to put pictures of smiling family members into groups, like in a game of gin.

Viv and I would go into Ma's bed and sip tea or snooze until we had to get dressed for school. Sometimes Uncle Cann had to travel to a factory in another town, and Viv would sleep with Ma all night.

I'd fallen back to sleep in my own little bed when Viv shook me—hard.

"Joy, Joy. Ma's still asleep. It's eight o'clock. We'll be late for school. Quick. Let's shout, 'Good morning, Ma! Good morning, Ma!' to wake her up."

I thought Ma was sleeping. Her mouth was open a little, but most grownups I'd seen slept with their mouths open. Ma's arm hung over the side of the bed and looked sort of heavy.

It was a bluish-grey colour, and the only difference from usual was that Ma's fingers were stretched out stiffly. Viv said Ma's hands and legs were cold. Much colder than usual.

Viv tried to put Ma's heavy hand back under the bedclothes, but it wouldn't go.

Every time she tried to move it, it flopped back.

I lay on her tummy to see if she was breathing and if her chest was going up and down. I listened at her lips. But there was nothing. My eyes were misty. We didn't know what to do.

Ma was dead.

Myrtle started howling. A long mournful howl. Viv and I howled as loud as Myrtle. We rushed over to the neighbours and told them what had happened. We asked them to get hold of Uncle Cann at work. One of the neighbours called the authorities. We went back to the house and waited with them. When we heard the sound of Uncle Cann's keys opening the front door, Myrtle, Viv, and I rushed to him. The four of us hugged as tears poured down our cheeks and onto our clothes.

"My dear little ones," sobbed Uncle Cann. "I'll make sure you are taken care of. In the meantime, I have two aunts who I know will look after you until everything is settled."

Later, the neighbours entered the house and said, "Pack up your haversacks. I'm afraid you'll have to move. Uncle Cann has to work. He can't look after you girls by himself."

Once again, our haversacks, full of our possessions, sat on the doorstep.

We waited and waited. Our minds were in a muddle. Everything had happened so quickly.

I couldn't play Happy Families anymore.

CHAPTER 10

WAS IT FAR ENOUGH?

Another billeting officer, one we'd never seen before, came to fetch us. She told us she couldn't find a billet for us at such short notice, but Uncle Cann had asked his two aunts if we could stay with them.

"They're old, so you two are going to have to be very good and very quiet. They're strict Baptists, so there'll be no music on the wireless or going to the pictures. And it's three times to church on Sundays."

I wondered why she'd spoken about going to the pictures. The only one we'd seen since the war started was Shirley Temple in *Bright Eyes,* which Viv liked but I didn't, and the only picture place, The Majestic, didn't let children in unless they were accompanied by an adult.

As for church, I wasn't sure how the Baptist service differed from a Methodist one. Perhaps they sang more hymns with different words. So far I had liked High Church best. It reminded me of Uncle Vicar and smelled of hayfields and fresh vegetables. It was cleaner and more friendly than the church the Shorts had made us attend. But there was no time for any more thoughts.

The billeting officer urged us to hurry. Her loud voice snapped, "Forward now!" Our black patent shoes click-clacked on the pavement as we marched.

She stopped in front of a small, narrow house, squished in the middle of a row of houses, a door and window on the ground floor and two small windows upstairs. No gate. No garden. No path. There was only crumbly clay bricks and weathered paint on the door and windowsills.

We never spoke about the dead body, Viv and I. Ma Cann's dead body. I didn't want to shut my eyes. I was certain I would dream about Ma Cann and the way she looked lying there with her eyes open and her arm dangling. Would I ever be able to close my lids and sleep again?

My eyes ached and smarted. Heavy weights seemed to be dragging my top eyelids down and I stumbled.

"Pick your feet up, girl. Look sharp. We're here."

The minute the door opened, I smelled death again. I looked at Viv and knew she did too. We froze on the doorstep. The smallest, thinnest, oldest woman I'd ever seen greeted us in a high, piping voice. Her face was crisscrossed with a thousand lines. The hard palms of the billeting officer pushed us from behind, and we fell into the front room, sending Uncle Cann's tiny aunty tumbling onto a couch.

"Steady, steady, steady," a voice cackled. It came from another body, one lying on a divan. "Don't knock Aunty Mabel over."

This time the cackle made the glass ornament on the sideboard jiggle and tinkle. I thought of Hansel and Gretel. My mouth went dry. Viv was biting her lips. We were both scared stiff.

We looked behind us. The billeting officer had left. We were alone in a room with two very old women. Alive. But for how long?

Then everything became blurry.

Later, I couldn't remember how things had happened, or in what order. I knew Viv and I were running and running and running as fast as we could. I couldn't keep up with her. I was breathless. The strap of one of my black patents came off. My white ankle sock was filthy, and there was a big hole in its toe. A blister on my heel was bleeding. My haversack felt like a hundred bricks on my back. And Viv was pulling me along.

"We can't stop yet. They'll catch us. C'mon, Joy. Take your other shoe off. It'll be easier." We were almost at the edge of the village. There was no pavement, only a grass verge, a shallow ditch, and a high hedge. My teacher had told me that in this county, all the hedges were hawthorn hedges. Their red berries made me feel bold and free and brave about running away.

A tall thistle stuck out of the hedge, its sharp points looking dangerous. I wondered if I should try to pick its long stem. It could help defend Viv and me when they came after us.

We read the white signpost on the grassy verge. The painted black letters said *Totteridge, 5 miles.*

I almost blurted out, "Let's totter on to Totteridge." I was glad I didn't. I got scared when Viv lost her temper. She kept telling me to grow up.

I knew I had to. I had to be braver. And not be scared of people.

I made a list of all the people I liked and loved and wasn't afraid of. I realized it was as long as our school register. At the top of the list were Mum and Dad. As I thought of them, big tears started coming.

"God! Don't start blubbering now. It's five miles to Totteridge. Let's totter on!"

Then I knew. My Viv could be funny when she was not cross with me, and I loved her even when I almost hated her. She was right at the top of the list, with Mum and Dad.

I heard a whirring noise. We looked behind. A small black van pulled to a stop.

"Get in, young 'uns. You've run far enough."

And that was how we were caught.

A man with a gruff voice shouted, coughed, and laughed. "I see you left your shoe for the ferrets."

A lady in a brown uniform shushed him and put her arm around me, and I fell asleep.

The next thing I knew we were being handed over to yet another billeting officer.

"Go with him. He'll take you to your new home," the lady officer said.

He told us his name was Brown. "Mr. Bill Brown, to be exact."

We'd never seen him before. He smelled awful.

I called him "B.O.," but not to his face.

"Listen 'ere. You two are giving me enough trouble. After I drop you off at the Youngs, I don't want never to see you again. D'you hear?"

Viv muttered, "And vicky verky."

I sniggered, hearing the echo of my father's voice. He had explained that "vicky verky" was a play on words from the Latin *vice versa*, which means opposite. How true that was; we didn't want to see the smelly officer again either.

Officer B.O.'s eyeballs blazed from their sockets.

My sniggering stopped. He took us to a nearby house.

We hoped these new foster parents would be familiar with children our age.

We were soon to discover they were not.

CHAPTER 11
PUB CRAWLERS

The yellow paint around the window of the house was shiny. I poked into its shininess.

My finger stuck there, making a dent.

A woman's voice snapped, "Take your finger off the window frame, child. The paint's hot. It'll crack if you finger it. These them then, Bill? Bring 'em in here. Your missus told me you were in a tight spot."

"Ta, Youngy, hafta' look for one more runaway. These two didn't get no further than the Totteridge signpost. I'll be off. See you at The Farmer's Rest later. Us 'uns'll all be there."

"Bye then, Bill. Have our drinks ready. Y'know how dry Fred gets. All that dust from the factory clogs his throat." As Officer Bill left, the woman looked us up and down.

I had never seen a woman like this before. Her face was narrow and pointy, her cheekbones stuck out and seemed as though they were piercing her skin, and her thin lips were outlined in a vibrant vermilion lipstick. She frightened me.

My first thought was, blood could drip from those lips at any moment.

Her peroxide-blonde hair was pulled back in a blue snood—one of those thick-knitted hairnets that look like shopping bags—and her body was thin and bony. When I looked hard at her body, my thoughts changed. Does she feel bony to Fred when he cuddles her? I wondered.

I was sure that those bones would dig into him.

"All right, you two; now come in and sit there while I tell you the rules. Wipe your feet first. I don't need extra work."

She pointed at two hard wooden chairs in the dark, narrow hallway. We sat and listened while she read the list. She read quickly, in a singsong voice.

"No staying inside when Mr. Young and me aren't home.

"No clean clothes except on Sunday.

"Help stir the boiler, wring the washing in the mangle, and hang the washing on the line after you get home from school on Mondays.

"No school kids allowed in our home.

"No more than three pieces of bread for tea and one cake or one biscuit.

"Don't talk in church."

Her speaking quickly made her English difficult to understand. Perhaps it was her pronunciation. She added, "And we go to church three times every Sunday, and so will you."

I said, in my most grownup voice, "Please, Mrs. Youngy, will you write those rules on a piece of paper so we can remember them?"

Quick as lightning, my face was slapped hard with a yellow duster. "You cheeky little bitch; that's enough lip from you. The name's Mrs. Young, and you're going to have to learn there's no answering back in my house."

Viv spoke pointedly. "She only wanted to get all the rules straight in her mind, Mrs. Young. She wasn't being rude. And our parents don't hit us, and I don't think you should."

"Huh. You don't think, don't ya? Well, you can bloody well think again. My father caned me. Fred's mother strapped him. And we'll do whatever we bloody well please to you snotty little Jew kids."

I closed my wet eyelids and imagined Viv and me running down High Street with everyone in the village chasing us like the Pied Piper of Hamelin.

But I knew we'd better not try to run away again.

When he handed us over to Mrs. Young, Officer B.O. had warned us, "Don't never try anything like this one more time or I'll hafta lock you up."

"We won't, will we, Joy? We don't want to be locked up. Oh no."

Viv had used her most sarcastic voice. He hadn't caught on and probably didn't know what sarcasm or irony meant.

There was a clatter at the door and a cheery call: "Is anyone at home? Did Bill bring us the two little 'uns?"

That was how we met Mr. Fred Young.

"I think he's going to be different from her," Viv whispered out of the corner of her mouth.

Mrs. Young was watching me, so I dared not answer.

Mr. Fred Young had a round, red face and watery blue eyes. He smiled at us. "Hello, you two. Look, Audrey, I'm all in and hafta have a bit of shut-eye before we go down to The Farmer's Rest. We'll take the girls with us. Give them their tea and get them ready."

Mrs. Young looked as though she was going to argue, but she must have changed her mind. Her lips closed in a straight thin line.

Audrey? I said to myself. Is she the Audrey Dad often joked about? The Little Audrey who laughed and laughed and laughed. She was the subject of popular jokes at the time. It didn't look to me like this Audrey ever laughed.

We soon discovered that Mrs. Audrey Young could laugh. A different kind of laughter—longer and higher. She laughed every night except Tuesdays and Sundays. Those were the only nights she and Mr. Fred didn't go to The Farmer's Rest.

On Mondays, Wednesdays, Thursdays, Fridays, and Saturdays she laughed from seven to eleven at night. Then, at five minutes past eleven on the dot, when the pub doors were closing, she laughed all the way up the street and into the house. She laughed as she pushed us up the stairs. She laughed as we fell onto the bed, shivering.

We never laughed. We forgot what it felt like.

All the hours and minutes between pub times, Mrs. Audrey Young was angry. Our mealtimes were nightmares. Breakfast, dinner, and high tea.

Three nightmares a day.

But the biggest nightmare was our first teatime.

The table was set, one plate with paper-thin bread slices scraped with a trace of margarine; a small container of jam and one of sugar; three tiny sponge-like "fairy" cakes; three small plates; and three teacups. When I held up my empty cup to the light, I could see right through it.

"You be careful with my bone china. It's my family's Wedgwood. It costs the earth. Now … hold the cup and cock your little finger up. I'll learn you to be ladies."

She passed the bread plate. We both took a triangle. It was so thin that mine fell apart. It all went into my mouth at once yet felt like nothing was there.

"Swallow silently," she hissed. "Close your mouths! Don't gulp! It's up to me, I suppose, to teach you manners. Don't you know not to make a noise when you eat? Chew like this! No one should hear you."

She showed us. We took another triangle of bread and tried to copy.

"Either sugar in your tea or jam on your bread. One or the other. Which do you want?"

We both started to answer. Her voice rose to a high pitch. She spluttered and then screamed, "I just told you, shut your mouths. Never speak with food in your mouth. I don't want to see that mess, and I don't want to hear your eating."

I wanted to make sense of it all but couldn't. I took tiny bites of the bread and tried not to chew. If I held it in my mouth and squashed it between my tongue and the roof of my mouth and then collected saliva to mush it up, maybe I could, with small throat movements, help it slither down into my tummy. I wished my tummy could talk proper words.

I'd ask it why it was always getting me into trouble by making funny noises.

If only I wasn't so hungry.

How could a throat make so much noise? It was painful. It felt as though there was a big iron gate at the top of my throat, like the ones they had in castles at the end of the moat. Those gates stopped the enemy from getting in.

Food had become my enemy. So had water and milk because drinking was worse.

When she left the table to get more boiling water for tea, I whispered to Viv, "Mrs. Young must be the only person in the world who can drink so no one can hear."

I thought I'd found the way she did it. I held the cup to my lips and tilted it, so it hardly let any tea escape. Sometimes that worked. Not always. Often it trickled from the corner of my lips.

"That's right. Dribble, you baby." Mrs. Young sneered.

I narrowed my eyes. Viv kicked me under the table. She didn't want me to get into trouble. Suddenly, my mouth tasted like burned-out fuse wire. The smell filled my nose and travelled into my head. Nothing was right. I was starving but couldn't eat or drink. Smelling, swallowing, and chewing were difficult. Noises and rumbles filled my tummy.

I was frightened.

I hated her.

I was never sure which day it was. Days and nights became mixed up. Viv seemed mixed up too. Her forehead was always wrinkled, and she blinked a lot.

It was the end of October, and the smell of burning leaves was the getting-ready-for-winter smell that I knew from our garden in London. Dad and Mum didn't feel so far away when that smell was in my nose.

Mrs. Young pushed us out the door early in the mornings to go to school.

It wasn't light yet but we didn't mind, even though we were at school before everyone else. We huddled by the door that had a sign that read "Entrance-Girls Only." Although the village school was different, we felt safe there. School lessons felt safe.

Nothing else felt safe.

I wondered if our London school was closed. Mr. Fred had heard somebody at his factory say that all the schools in London were closed. He said the war was already seventy-five days old. I knew that. I'd counted every day. When I told Viv, she said that it felt like seventy-five years.

Every night Mr. Fred turned up the sound on the wireless when the six o'clock news came on. I tried not to listen too much. I didn't want to know. And yet I did. I desperately wanted to know what was going on with the war.

A few days earlier, a teacher had told us our very own London teachers had been called up. "Mr. Jones and Mr. Walker are fine men, and they have gone to fight for our country. Mr. Jones has gone into the Welsh Guards, and Mr. Walker is in the RAF."

Even the kids in Class One knew those letters meant Royal Air Force.

I loved Mr. Jones. I didn't want him to be in the war.

After that news, the teacher said, "You kids will be sent to another school soon—there's no room for you evacuees here. Anyway, nearly all of you who came to our village have gone back to London. Good thing too. You've given us lots of trouble. Now, I don't mean you two." She pointed at us. "You're bright enough. You'll probably get into the grammar school."

I looked at Viv. She looked at me.

Moving, moving, always moving. Nothing stayed still.

My legs and feet were full of pins and needles jabbing me. I wished my ankles had wings like Apollo. I knew what I'd use them for: flying home to see Mum and Dad.

Some days, after our teacher bellowed, "Class dismissed," some of the village kids would ask us to come and play Kiss-Chase. They played every day in the fields behind the school.

Viv liked kissing boys, but I didn't want to. I thought it would feel mushy. Viv said I was too choosy.

One of Mrs. Young's rules was "Straight back home after school" because we had to have tea, wash the dishes, and be ready for The Farmer's Rest. The Youngs insisted we go even when we promised we'd stay in bed all the time they were out. They both got cross and said we had a bloody nerve to ask that.

We couldn't decide what was more horrid: trying to eat and drink without being heard, going to the pub, or seeing them "one over the eight."

We'd never seen drunken people before. We didn't know their faces got so red. Drunken people said silly things in funny voices. Mrs. Audrey Young was the silliest of the lot. It was hard not to laugh. Mum and Dad drank, but they called themselves celebration drinkers. They drank wine every Friday night to welcome the Sabbath, they drank at all the Jewish holidays, our Yom Tovs, and they drank champagne at weddings. Daddy celebrated his team's win at cricket. Then he would have a tankard of draught beer. Draught beer was very stinky.

Before the war, when we went on picnics and bicycle rides, we would sit in the gardens of country pubs, and Dad would buy us a drink each. Two tall glasses of Tizer, the orange drink with fizzy bubbles that tingled on the tongue. Viv and I worried a lot about Mum and Dad. We didn't tell them about The Farmer's Rest, or Mrs. Young's laughing. Nor about the cruel things she said about us. And Jews. We didn't want to worry them. We were worried enough about the nights.

Every night we shivered outside the pub from seven until eleven when the landlord shouted, "Time, gentlemen, please." It wasn't easy to clear the pub. Drinkers wanted to empty their glasses to the last drop and stay with their mates by the warmth of the fire. "Out, you lot, it's nearly quarter past!"

We froze at night. Our teeth chattered so hard our jaws ached.

We didn't have any winter clothes. Our skirts and jackets were thin. Even with their tops turned up, our ankle socks couldn't keep our legs warm. Our shoes pinched our toes, especially the big toes, making us hobble. The headmistress had noticed. She shouted out in front of the class, "You two Londoners, your clothes are getting threadbare. Ask your foster parents to buy you some warm things."

We knew enough not to ask.

Mrs. Audrey Young complained every day about the money she was paid for looking after us. "Not enough to feed a flea. How the hell d'they think I can buy anything with this pittance? I'll be in the poorhouse before I know it."

Viv grinned. "The perfect place for her. I'll bet she'd hear lots of belching there—and noises coming from you know where." She pointed to her bum.

"Viv!" I was embarrassed.

"Oh, Joy! Stop being such a little prude. It's only a joke."

And I realized that's what we had to do—the only way to keep our spirits up was to joke.

Viv kidded easily, but I had to try hard to make it work.

The lights inside the pub looked cheery from where we stood. We heard snatches of the pub talk—"Hello"—"What happened at work today?"—"Did you catch the BBC news?"

"Let's pretend we're cosy in there with them," said Viv.

But we weren't. And we knew it. And the wind was bitter.

It felt like a carving knife cutting into our bodies. My legs were purple, and Viv's were deep blue. We rubbed them, and it burned our hands until they stung, so we stopped. Our noses dripped and dripped.

Viv teased, "Remember when the washer was worn on our bathroom tap at home and Dad fixed it? Your nose is dripping nonstop, and your face is as long and droopy as our tap. Come here, Tappy, let's cuddle."

I knew she was trying to make me forget that we wouldn't be in bed for hours, but it didn't work. I kicked the pavement. I kicked the pub door and hurt my aching toes. "I hate this village and all the people in it!"

Viv tried to reason with me. "You didn't hate Uncle Vicar, or Aunty Mabel, or Uncle Cann, or Ma Cann, so stop snivelling."

"Viv, can I still love Ma Cann? Will she know that I do, now that she's dead? Why won't the billeting officer tell me whether Uncle Vicar is alive or dead and if Ma Cann is in heaven?"

Viv didn't say anything. I wondered if she knew the answer. I wasn't going to ask again. I didn't care if I ever knew. But the more I thought about it, I realized I was lying to myself.

I did care. I did want to know.

We huddled by the door, trying to catch the smoky air as drinkers went in and out.

We heard what the pub goers muttered as they passed us.

"Look at these kids, Pete. Poor things. Should be in bed; it's gone nine."

"Where's their mams?"

"Go fetch 'em, Lil. It's freezing here."

Youngy came out. "You kids been telling tales?"

She boxed my ears with her knuckles. A whistling sound zinged in my head; both ears felt on fire. I kicked her ankle and she squealed. I was glad.

Mr. Fred appears. "Wotcher doin', Luvvy? Gals bothrin' ya?"

"Bleedin' bitch kicked me, Fred." Her scream brought other drinkers, out wondering about the commotion.

The man called Pete slapped Mr. Young's shoulder. "C'mon Fred. Let's get back inside. It's too bloody cold out 'ere—'snuff to freeze the balls off a brass monkey."

"Nah, no dirty talk in front of the kids," one onlooker commented.

"Crikey, Edie, they know what balls is," Mr. Fred said as he steered his wife back into the pub. But I didn't know.

"Do you, Viv?" I asked, turning to her.

My ears still burned. I hoped Youngy hadn't burst my eardrum. Viv and I wanted to get away from The Farmer's Rest. We decided to run to the park. It was not too far from the pub, but not too near either. It was darkish and full of shadows. We sang in loud voices wanting to be brave. My ear still ached and it affected my voice, making it gravelly. The moon shined, partly hidden behind the clouds, and the shadows stretched out spookily.

"Viv, there's a man waving to us. See, some people in this village are friendly. Look. He's holding something in his hand."

The man started to run toward us. He was getting nearer. Nearer.

"What is it?" I asked. "What is that long thing he's holding?"

Viv suddenly grabbed my hand and pulled me.

"Run, Joy. Run the fastest you've ever run in your life."

She pulled so hard I thought my arm was going to come out of its socket.

We ran and ran. My head ached, there was a stitch in my side, and I couldn't breathe.

Viv panted as she pulled me along. She looked over her shoulder. "He's shouting at us, but he's stopped running. Quick. Here's the road to the pub."

It took a long time for my heart to stop its thumps.

"Joy, rub your cheeks. You're as pale as a ghost. Do it like this." She lightly pinched her cheeks to show me. "Listen! We won't say anything about this to anyone. Not a word. We'll get into more trouble than we're in already."

She put her arms around me and gave me a kiss. She didn't do this often. We squeezed into a small space beside the pub's doors. All the dogs peed there, but at least the wind couldn't make us shiver there.

When the war ends, I'll ask my dad about balls, I thought. And why did that man chase us? And why was he holding a thick stick? Was he going to hit us?

I knew Dad would tell me one day.

But we never told Mum and Dad what had happened that day in the park. We didn't want to worry them.

CHAPTER 12
BUBBLE AND SQUEAK

E very day, the minute he opened the front door, Mr. Fred said, "Gawd, I'm tired."

He worked very hard at his factory. It was hush-hush. He wouldn't tell us exactly what he did, but he gave hints. I thought he made bombs to drop on Germany. Viv wasn't sure. He had big hands and made mechanical tools in his work shed. Perhaps he fixed aeroplanes.

He said, "I'll probably be called up soon but may not pass the medical because of my flat feet."

I tried not to laugh when I saw him walk. He waddled like Charlie Chaplin's hobo.

We liked Mr. Fred. He was polite when he spoke to us. Except when he went to the pub, his manner was gentle.

On Tuesdays, Fred Young went to the Working Man's Club. There, the members collected stamps from all over the world. Before he went to the club, Mr. Fred would sit us down at the dining room table and show us his stamp album. Despite his stubby hands, his fingers were nimble. He could sort even the tiniest stamp in his collection into its correct country.

On Tuesday nights, Fred ate his dinner at the Working Man's Club. He told us he was a meat-and-potatoes man and enjoyed a nice meal at the club. On those nights, Youngy cooked bubble and squeak for us. She wanted to cook something that was quick and easy to prepare and only used vegetables: "Meat's wasted on you kids." Her bubble and squeak was so different from the way our mum made it.

I loved the way Mum made it. She would add mushrooms and onions to the Brussels sprouts and potatoes. Dad said, "I can hear the squeak all the way in the front room, and that's a long way from the kitchen!"

I'll never forget Youngy's bubble and squeak. Youngy dolloped two huge serving spoonfuls onto our plates. There were no potatoes, no Brussels sprouts, no mushrooms. It smelt like manure. It looked like swill. Chunks and chunks of deep orangey-grey things that looked like pig's tails and strips of pale yellow and white cabbage filled our plates.

I stared at it. My eyes were on stalks. The lump in my throat felt as big as a football.

"Start, you two. When you've finished, it's up to bed. I gotta have my peace and quiet. Now—down that food. I don't wanna see nothing left on those plates."

Silence.

"I can't eat it, Mrs. Young," Viv said, trying not to upset the woman glaring at us.

"Neither can I. I don't like those things," I whispered carefully.

"You bloody well will eat it. My swede and parsnip squeak's famous. It's my Fred's favourite. He eats swedes mashed, boiled, and roasted. He says it's the turnip's cousin. So shut yer traps and get on with it. You'll sit there until yer done."

I played with my knife and fork. So did Viv. I cut the end of the grey tail-looking thing and a corner of a chunk. I bit it. Ugh! It tasted like it looked. Swill.

I wanted to spit it out. Viv did.

Youngy gave her a swat on the head. We said nothing. We sat. And sat. I cried. I couldn't help it. I heaved big sobs. I sounded like a horse shuddering.

"That's enough, you little kike!" she barked.

She grabbed my fork and forced the swill into my mouth. My lips opened. I swallowed with a gulp, and down my throat it went.

"Now you," she said in menacing voice as she turned to Viv.

"I'll do it myself," Viv replied. And slowly, slowly Viv swallowed.

I copied her. I swallowed and swallowed. We made ourselves swallow without tasting. Without feeling. We blanked everything out. We took as long as we dared.

Youngy glared and glared, and when we were finally done, she pushed us up the stairs. "Not a sound. Not one bleedin' sound do I want to hear from you!"

We didn't make a sound. We tried to be as quiet as church mice. We laid our heads on our pillows and tried to sleep.

I woke to the strangled sound of heaves and the smell of pigswill. Viv was clutching her throat with one hand and her tummy with the other. She couldn't stop vomiting. It kept coming and coming and big chunks of orange and grey were all over the eiderdown.

I didn't know what to do. I felt helpless.

I heard Youngy storming up the stairs.

"Viv, stop. Please stop. She's coming," I pleaded.

Suddenly, she was there, her face distorted by rage. She was screaming, swearing, and hitting Viv. Youngy had something in her hand, and Viv was yelping, her nose and lip bleeding.

I snatched a wooden hand mirror from the dressing table, swung my arm up, and hit the hand mirror on the iron bedstead. The glass came out and smashed into smithereens.

There was sick and blood and broken glass everywhere.

The eiderdown was covered with the mess.

Youngy didn't stop.

She bashed and bashed my Viv's head and shoulders with a wooden hairbrush and thumped her back from top to bottom. She bashed me too.

I thought Youngy had lost her mind.

I screamed as loud as I could, "Mr. Fred! Mr. Fred! Help us!"

Mr. Fred came when I called. He quickly pulled his wife into their bedroom. I heard the door slam and the key turn. We were still crying when he came back. He tried to calm us as he washed the blood from our faces, put arnica on our cuts and bruises, and dabbed our ears with lavender water. He changed our sheets and pillowcases and found a clean cover for the bed.

He didn't leave us alone until we had fallen back to sleep.

The next morning he made our breakfast and gave us a note to take to our headmistress.

When we arrived at school, our class teacher showed us what Mr. Fred had written: "I think the girls should be moved. They're not bad girls, but my wife is under the weather. I have packed all their things. Please tell the billeting officer we won't be taking any more foster children."

When she took us to the headmistress to give her the note, our teacher made us take off our vests to show our wounds.

It is hard to hide swollen lips and bruised backs.

We were shaky all day, so they allowed us to rest in the Teachers' Room.

We slept on and off most of the day.

When school had finished and all the children had gone home, another billeting officer arrived. He said, "We know you're good girls, but we can't find anybody who'll take two sisters. We've found two places willing to take you, but you'll have to separate."

"Separate? We can't!" we cried.

We clutched each other for support.

"We have to stick together!" we said emphatically.

"Listen," he said kindly. "These foster homes are on opposite sides of the street. They face each other. It's a narrow street."

It became as wide as the Atlantic Ocean.

CHAPTER 13

BEST OF THE BRICKYARD

At the billeting office, we were handed to our new billeting officer. She smiled and quickly escorted us over to our new homes. She took Viv first. I watched as she knocked with a huge brass doorknocker. A posh woman opened the door, nodded her head, pulled Viv inside, and sharply shut the door. I felt sick. Was this the way it was going to be? Were we ever going to be together again?

"I'm sure you'll see her later," the officer said as we crossed the road.

I wasn't so sure. I felt desperate. The wind whistled through my body. My head felt fuzzy. It was if we were being swallowed into an unknown world.

The billeting officer who held my arm tightly was talking. I caught only a few words. "Bricklayer … daughter Betty … simple family." I tripped on a jutting-up pavestone. The billeting officer stopped me from falling flat on my face.

"Goodness, child, concentrate. I don't believe you're hearing a word I'm saying. You're about to meet your new foster mum. I told her you're a bright one. Don't show me up."

She led me down a wide alley. I heard *crunch, crunch*. I looked down, gasped. We were walking on round knobs of cinder, generally used to start a coal fire in the grate. The black powdery soot turned my ankle socks dark grey. The officer's lisle stockings were covered in soot too. I read the painted wooden sign nailed into the wall: Bricklayer Yard to the right—Coal Yard to the left.

Where was she taking me? I wondered. Was I going to live with a chimney sweep's family?

A wooden shed was in the coal yard, and a small brick building was at the entrance of the other yard, but no house was in sight. Before we reached either yard, we stopped at a door below the wooden sign. I hadn't noticed it. She lifted the doorknocker and let it fall hard. It sounded like a heavy roll of thunder with a bouncing echo.

From behind the door I heard giggling and laughing. A cheery voice said, "Careful, child. Don't hurt yourself."

The door opened. A small woman wearing a striped pinafore appeared.

Beside her was round-faced girl with large brown eyes who dropped onto the gleaming white doorstep, lifted her paws, and begged like a dog. "Woof! Woof! I'm Betty," the little girl said.

A gale of giggles followed as she stood up and clasped her arms around the pinafore.

The woman was tiny. All I could see was her head and feet. Was she "doggy Betty's" mother? She looked old to me. Her hair was a black and grey mixture and was cut short, right above her ears. They matched the colour of the bow in Betty's hair: bright red.

I thought her ears must be cold.

The officer pushed me forward. "Hello, Mrs. Downey. Hello, Betty. Here she is, Mrs. Downey. This is Joy. Now say hello, Joy."

I said hello and tried to make my voice sound friendly. But as I said my name it came out abruptly, sounding unfriendly and a bit lukewarm. I made amends by grinning at Betty, patted her head, and said, "Good doggie, nice doggie."

She giggled and begged again.

"Welcome. This is our home. It's not fancy like some have, but I hope you'll be happy with us." She smiled. Mrs. Downey's voice was soft and easy to hear. She spoke with what my dad calls "a soft burr." He said it's the way people in the country talk. It was gentle to listen to.

"Come in, both of you. Betty will show you where you will be sleeping, and us grownups will have a little talk down here."

"Sorry, Mrs. Downey. I can't stay," said the billeting officer as she rushed down the alley. "It's nearly teatime, and my two boys come home from school ready to eat a horse."

A black, sooty cloud rose. Mrs. Downey pulled me in. "Silly woman. The coal dust is flying all over. She'd've had us looking like chimney sweeps if we'd stayed out there much longer. Now, little puppy dog, show Joy where she she'll sleep and where she can put her belongings."

Mrs. Downey looked at my fallen-over haversack. Noticing my sad face she said, "I can see you don't have too much, and that's good because our home is small and we're cramped inside. It used to be a shop. A chemist's."

Mrs. Downey pointed to the front room where the chemist kept his bottles and jars, all shapes and sizes. "You can play with them and pretend you're the chemist's wife. I pickle eggs in some of the larger jars now the war's on."

I sniffed and smelled something but was not certain what it was. Was it purple potassium permanganate, or the stronger smell of iodine? Mum used to undo the brown bottle with a brush inside the top and paint my grazed knees. Yellow iodine hurt your eyes but not half as much hurting your wounds. Mum would draw a face on the wound to make me laugh and forget the stinging.

Betty tugged my hand. "C'mon, c'mon. Mummy's got more bottles in the cellar, but let's go upstairs. I'll show you where your bed is." She giggled and pulled me forward. "This way to our upstairs."

She went to the wall, lifted a latch, and opened a door. It was hard to see how the door fit into the wall. It was almost hidden. In front of us was a flight of stairs. It was very dark. The door slammed behind us. I couldn't see in front of my nose. The stairs were steep and wooden, and Betty's hard-soled shoes went click-clack. It was enclosed like a tunnel and her click-clacks echoed as loud as a Morse code message. I pretended it was a message for me: "Home soon. Home soon. Home soon." I decided then and there I was not going to stay long. Even if the Downeys did turn out to be kind.

Betty was so excited I thought I was on a playground roundabout, twisting this way and that. I felt giddy and clutched the wooden banister.

"Round this way, no, not that way, this way round here." She showed me a passageway that led from the parents' room at one end toward a closed door at the other. I was certain I would find a small room there just for me. A room where I could be alone. A room where I could dream of London. And of home.

I ran forward and pulled the door open, as Betty screamed with laughter when I gasped.

In front of me was a huge lavatory bowl, bright white and round, with a long, thick chain hanging down from the cistern above it. Dangling at the end of the chain was a penguin, knitted in black and white wool. He had buttons for eyes, and his flippers were sewn over and over with black embroidery thread.

"I tied my penguin on the chain. His name is Percy. He'll help you pull hard. Mummy says this is for you and Daddy to use at night. We have our chamber potties. Mummy warms mine by the fire. She told me that the rest of the time all the grownups have to use our outdoor lav. It's down the lane. No one can see you from the lane. They can only hear you if you're farting."

My eyes stretched wide. They smarted.

Betty saw my surprise and peered closely. "Daddy says that word a lot. He farts a lot too. He calls the lav the bog. I'm going to the bog. It's his joke."

I tried to smile, but I was not going to pee during the night.

Behind us, covering part of the wall, was a curtain hanging from the ceiling to the floor. Betty pulled the curtain as the brass hooks squealed their way along its rod.

"There's your room." She giggled again.

My eyes stretched once more. It was not a room at all, merely a small alcove with a tiny window and a saggy bed whose middle touched the floor. No chest of drawers. No wardrobe. No light to read by. No room to swing a cat. Nothing.

My heart sank.

Betty patted the eiderdown and stroked her cheek with its satin edge. "Isn't it pretty? It's the one I chose. Mummy says that as soon as Daddy gets his bonus, she is going to find a dresser. We'll keep it in our room 'cos it can't fit here. No room here." Betty laughed.

I hoped she would stop giggling soon.

"That's the wall hook to hang your best dress, but you'll have to keep your stuff in your haversack. C'mon, it's too cold to stay here. Let's go downstairs and play."

And play was what we did. Every day when I returned from school, Betty was waiting for me with her dolls, her metal cows, pigs, and sheep with their painted colours chipped away, her crayons, and her big, pleading eyes.

"Draw me a picture. No. Let's play house. No. Tell me a story. Please, please."

I never said no. I thought that if I did, I might be sent away, and then where would I go?

I knew I couldn't go home to Mum and Dad yet. They were both doing war work, and the kids at school said bombs fell on London every night. Every time I thought about that I held my breath and pulled my tummy in until it hurt. Sometimes I scratched my wrists so deep they bled.

Bit by bit I got used to the Downeys, used to the different foods: smelly cabbage slopping in water, burnt toast and burnt porridge for breakfast, fried bread for supper with fried bacon. I only pretended to eat it at first, but then it smelled so good that I tried it and liked it. I hoped Mum and Dad wouldn't mind that I ate *traif.*

Mrs. Downey said I could call her Aunty or Mum.

I chose Aunty Downey. Mr. Downey joked that I could call him Dee.

That short name seemed to fit.

Some days Aunty Downey would bring cakes and doughnuts back from her job. She cleaned a bakery every day. Her uncle Teddy was the baker and owned the shop. He was a kind man, fat and jolly, and was always covered in flour looking as white as a ghost. He let me watch him mix buns, cottage loaves, biscuits, and best of all, doughnuts with jam in the middle. He would set earthenware bowls in front of where he stood to work. They held the ingredients for his recipes: flour, fat, eggs, salt, sugar, and yeast. He filled an old beat-up kettle with water to have ready when he needed to sprinkle the flour to knead the dough. He worked as near as possible to the huge kiln that roared ferociously, ready to perform its duties. Uncle Teddy stoked the kiln himself, cleverly moving between the coke-filled coal shuttle and shovelling it into a cavernous kiln. His hands moved quickly. I thought he was a white-faced magician who liked performing tricks.

He beamed. "One day I'll teach you how to knead the dough. Watch carefully while I take several handfuls of flour, shake a few sprinkles from the kettle's spout, and make a pile on my kneading board. Soon I'll have a ball of dough to punch down."

He sounded like a warrior but looked like a chubby clown. I was glad. He held the ball, folded it, and with the heels of both hands he rocked back and forth, back and forth. As he kneaded I could see how the dough was forming. It looked like elastic.

"I think she's pugged enough," he said as he mopped the drops of sweat that ran down his cheeks. "It's got to feel like a sponge and spring when you touch it. You've seen one of those yellow seawater sponges of young Betty's. I expect you need muscles and energy. Do you think you're ready?"

I knew he was joking. I was skinny. Viv was skinnier.

I wished she was with me.

She was the one in our family who liked recipes and cooking.

Uncle Teddy smoked Wild Woodbines non-stop. He used to flick the ash off the end of his cigarette and let it fall onto whatever he was baking. I wondered what happened to the ash—all mixed up with the ingredients. I noticed and he giggled. "Don't tell."

Uncle Teddy helped Aunty Downey a lot. He knew she was short of money, and he slipped bank notes and coins into her ledger when his sister, Granny Shorter, wasn't looking.

He would stop her from speaking unkindly to me. "That's enough, sister. Mind your mouth."

In his friendly way he would rub a hand on Dee's shoulder, not bothered by Dee's dirty work clothes. Dee was dirty when he came home from work. His clumpy boots were muddy, and his trousers and shirt were covered with hard cement. Aunty Downey made him take off his clothes in the scullery.

"Strip to your underclothes," she said, "and I'll scrub your feet."

She brought his outer clothes to Betty and me, and we picked off the lumps of cement and threw them into a blue enamel bowl. It made a good clunky sound and we laughed.

Dee was kind and I liked him. He loved Betty, hugged her and kissed her and ruffled her hair when she sat on his lap. He ruffled my hair sometimes. One thing I didn't like were the nights he went to the pub. When he came home he had to pee a lot. I put my head under the covers so I couldn't see or hear him when he went by my bed. He belched and farted and I could hear and smell it all. The eiderdown and covers over my head didn't help one bit.

Aunty Downey's hands were always red and rough from scrubbing dirty clothes in cold water. I wished she didn't have to work so hard. I liked the way she looked at me with her cheeks crinkling. I liked the way she let me stroke her fingers. I even liked the way she made shepherd's pie. All crispy and burnt on top.

Everything changed when her mother, Granny Shorter ("Shorty"), came back from a long stay at Uncle Teddy's home.

She hated me the minute she saw me.

I wasn't sure why.

She told tales about me all the time, saying them loud enough for me to hear. "Look what that London brat's done now. Left her bed unmade. Thinks you have nothing better to do than wait on her. You just leave it undone, Mabel."

"Left all that good cabbage on her plate. Tried to hide the bacon under it. Thinks she comes from the Ritz, she does."

"Those Jew kids should go back to where they came from. This war's all because of them anyway."

Aunty Downey stuck up for me. "Hush up, Mother. She's a good kid. She's good with our Betty. You've seen Jews before but I haven't, and Joy's mother writes friendly letters. She's going to come down as soon as she can. I know you don't like the way the Jews shout in the market, but all stall-owners shout in the market. Stop it, Mother. Be Christian."

Granny said, "Hrrumph." First time I'd heard Granny Shorter lost for words.

Pretending to be Christian hadn't helped me. One thousand and eight hundred minutes Viv and I had been in chapels and churches. Trying to block out the words. Trying not to say the name "Jesus." My head ached three times a day on Sundays.

I felt guilty. Guilty all the time.

Not only about praying to "Jesus", but about everything. About missing Mum. About wishing I could help with the war.

Was it my fault? Was it because I was a Jew?

I wished I could be silly and giggly like Betty. I couldn't giggle.

Uncle Cann had tried to help me. I pushed thoughts of Uncle and Ma Cann away. I cried a lot, even though I tried not to. Shorty called me a cry-baby, and so did Viv. I was cross with them both. I didn't think Viv liked me any more. She used to like me most of the time, but even before the war she was mean to me and I was horrid to her.

I wondered if life was easier if you were a mean person. Mean people always seemed to get their way.

One day Betty asked me to tell her a story about Viv. I started telling her all the fun we had as sisters: about using our Singer treadle cover as a boat, about giggling in bed when Dad yelled at us to be quiet, about dressing up in gaudy ostrich feathers from our dress-up hat box.

As I was telling, Betty was laughing, I realized how much I loved Viv. I wished we were still together, but I knew there wasn't enough room for us both at the Downeys'.

The billeting officer had said everyone was fed up with the war and the cockney kids, but all I knew was that half of me was cut off. I missed Viv, even though I was, in a way, an older sister myself to Betty. The officer had placed Viv in a house across the street with a family called the Fitzgeralds. Aunty Downey said the Fitzgeralds were well off and owned a huge posh house spic and span inside and out. They had a girl from a farm to clean and cook for them. I asked Aunty Downey to tell me more about the Fitzgeralds.

The way she talked about them made me worried for Viv. I didn't know why I felt so uncomfortable.

Aunty Downey let me call on Viv on Saturdays and gave me money for us to go roller-skating, with enough left over for a fizzy drink. Whenever I called on Viv, Mrs. Fitzgerald seemed to be cold and unkind. I hardly saw Mr. Fitzgerald, but I sensed Viv did not like him. I wondered what they were doing to her. Viv's behaviour seemed to be changing. She was irritable with me much of the time. I wondered if this was because they often confined her to her room without supper, and she was hardly ever allowed out of the house. How did they speak to her? Did they abuse her with words? Or worse?

Whenever I saw Mr. Fitzgerald speak, his eyes narrowed with mistrust. With his lips pursed, it was as though he was judging Viv's every move. I thought he seemed capable of physical violence. It made me want to scream. I needed to help Viv get out of there. I wasn't sure who was more cruel—Mr. Fitzgerald or his wife. I hated them both for how they treated Viv, and I was filled with fear for my sister's safety.

One Saturday, I went across the street to see Viv. I knocked five times on their doorknocker shaped like a lion's face. An angry voice called out, "Never knock that hard again. Never."

I waited and waited for ages. The door opened a crack, and Viv slunk out with her head down.

I could see she'd been crying. She wouldn't let me hug her, and I couldn't reach her face to kiss her. I wondered how she got those bruises on her legs.

"C'mon. Let's go," she whispered. She ran ahead. By the time I caught up with her, she was blinking her eyes and clenching her hands. "Silly sods. Stupid stuck-up snobs. Snot up their noses, all of them."

"Viv. What's the matter? What happened when I knocked? You look funny doing that. Your eyes are disappearing into your head." My laugh turned into a snort and then tears. "Don't cry, Viv. Please don't. I'm frightened."

"Cry-baby," she called me. "You wouldn't last a minute with the Fitzgeralds. Anyway, I'm going back to London. The stupid, stupid school expelled me. I'm leaving as soon as Mum sends the bus fare. And don't stand there with your mouth gaping. You look like a fool. Put your tongue in. Only slow kids do that."

I was boiling. I saw red. I was so jealous. I wanted to punch her arm hard. Why was she allowed to go home and not me? How did she get expelled? I'd do whatever she did. I'd get expelled.

Viv told me she had written a note in class, breaking class-rule number one. The scrawled note on a crumbled piece of paper had been intercepted on its journey to another student. It revealed that "Miss B. was a boring bitch."

Viv had been sent back to the Fitzgeralds within the hour, accompanied by a prefect with a typed letter sealed with red wax addressed to her foster mother. Viv told me the Fitzgeralds had punished her severely for being expelled.

Our mum soon came and took Viv to a doctor who said her health was at risk. The next thing I knew, Viv was back in our parents' home in London. I was devastated. Why did they leave without me?

We were separated again. At the same time, I felt jealous. My stomach was in knots, and jealousy overtook all else until I came to my senses.

I worried about my sister and my family in war-torn London. I worried about the bombs falling.

Perhaps we'll be bombed here too, I thought. Air raids were happening. Heavy ones. Over every part of the country. I thought it was peculiar. We were evacuated from London to escape the bombing, yet here the sirens wailed every night. As the sirens sounded, German bombers droned overhead.

Each night was the same.

When the sirens sounded, we scrambled to the air-raid shelter in the cellar.

I liked the Downeys' cellar, although it puzzled me. It smelled different. Old. Haunted. Could people be buried here? It was large, hiding many nooks and crannies. The stone steps down turned round and round in circles, like spiral staircases that led up to church belfries. After turning some of the steps, there were ledges set into the walls. One ledge went deeper than the rest. That's where I was supposed to sleep. Aunty Downey tried to make it comfy by lining it with old blankets, but it was hard and hurt my bones. Nearest to my ledge was an entrance to a small room.

"That's where they used to keep the poisons," Betty said. "Guess whose bed is in there?"

I grinned and so did she. We both knew.

"Me and Mummy and Daddy havta go all the way down—there's a'normous flat part of the floor we fit on. I sleep in the middle. I'm not scared. Daddy says I'm too big to be scared. Sometimes he grumbles that I take up too much room. It's not fair that Shorty has her own room."

"It's like a rabbit warren, Betty. Where are the cuddly bunnies?"

Betty giggled. I didn't mind her giggles now.

I thought that in some ways I might be growing up, because I realized that when you liked someone, you don't mind when they do things you used to hate. The opposite was true too. When you can't stand someone, the way they look and the way they talk, even the way they eat sends you up the wall. That's the way I felt about Granny Shorty. I decided I was going to get my own back on her.

I put my plan into action. I invented a language made up of nonsense sounds that could almost have been real words. I made my voice louder and softer as I started speaking the nonsense language.

My teacher in London used to say, "I think I'll see your name in the papers one day. Joy Abrahams—famous actress. You know about rhythm and pacing; that's what makes you a good reader."

I knew nothing about rhythm or pacing except in country dancing, but the meaning of words seemed to come to me by themselves. I acted them out every night.

Softly, through clenched teeth, I said, "Gho, ghu waja." My voice died away. I moaned and moaned.

Shorty moaned too. "Make that little bitch shut up. She's driving me up the wall."

"Now, Mother, she can't help it. It's in her sleep. She—"

"Now, don't you make no excuses for the brat. She's doing it on purpose. 'Zhoo wawa,' whatever that means."

Granny Shorty couldn't imitate me very well even in her most sarcastic voice. "She does that once more and she'll get the feel of my foot. I want to kick the talk out of her."

Dee stopped her rant with, "Now, Granny, keep your shirt on."

I stifled a snort. I could just see Granny in a nightshirt.

My last words, in deep bass, were, "Fugral. Chrase."

"That's it. Enough of her twaddle. I'm goin' up to my bed."

"Now, Mother, don't take on so."

Up she went, muttering and sniffing. That's another thing she did—sniffed because her nose dripped constantly. I watched her through slitted eyelids and gloated. I'd won. Inside, my chest felt different. All puffed up. Like a rooster before it started crowing. I fell asleep.

In the morning, when we left the cellar, I wondered what Shorty would say to me. I didn't have to wait long.

"Look at me, yer little bitch. No sleep for me last night with all yer shenanigans."

She did look awful. Her eyeballs were as red as the outside of a radish, and the bags underneath them were droopier than ever.

"It's all that talking yer doin'. The racket is fit to raise the dead."

"Don't talk about the dead, Granny," Aunty Downey said over breakfast. "You'll frighten our Betty."

Granny Shorty snarled back. "It'll hafta' be her or me. Either she goes or I go."

"Granny, you know you can't go and live with your brother. You lived with Teddy and Marge for six months, and poor Marge almost had a nervous breakdown."

I began to feel ashamed and almost said, "I'm sorry I kept you awake." But the words stuck in my throat. It was tit for tat, if she started being nicer to me, I would be nicer to her.

Over time, a funny thing happened. I didn't know who started it first, but one day Granny Shorter and I had a truce. The cellar no longer echoed with my nonsense language, and Granny Shorter's snores bounced up and down the cellar stairs.

There was nowhere to play outside the Downey home. The entrance to the coal yard had too many pitfalls, lumps of coke, and a few bits and pieces of sharp anthracite. If we collected a bucketful of the coal, the foreman would give us a shilling, but there never seemed to be enough to fill a bucket so we played games instead.

Once when I was practicing my double Dutch in the coal yard, I fell. I tried to make my hands turn the skipping rope double time and my legs jump high and stay there, but it didn't work. The fall was a hard one. It took my breath away. The soot and cinder left black striped scars on my knees for more than five weeks, and I never did manage to do the double Dutch. Betty and I were able to scrawl a hopscotch grid on the yard entrance. We used a chunk of chalk we had found in a farmer's field, and it showed all the lines and figures clearly. Betty couldn't draw her numbers yet. I used to put my hand on top of hers and guide her grid drawing.

We would get the giggles, especially when we had to draw four, five, or eight. The circles looked squiggly, and the straight lines shot off at odd angles.

Aunty D. would call us in her high, tinny voice: "Teatime. Teatime."

Every day she would have something special for tea: a jelly doughnut or jellyroll with cream slathered in its circles. Uncle Teddy sent them for his great-niece Betty and for "the cockney kid."

Aunty D. was worried about Betty. When I was drying the dishes one night she whispered to me, "Betty can't do sums and isn't learning her letters. You help her. She loves you. You're like a big sister to her, and her dad and me are grateful."

A tear rolled down Aunty D.'s cheek. I wanted to tell her I was sure Betty would learn in the end, that she was enthusiastic and eager like a cocker-spaniel puppy.

"Of course I'll help her until I go back to my own home."

I didn't want Aunty D. to think I was going to stay in her house forever. In one way I liked being thought of as a big sister, and I liked the thought of being loved by someone who wasn't a member of my own family. But I missed my Viv and missed the things we did together—reciting poems and singing songs, and doing athletic things, especially the Flying Porpoise.

We'd seen a picture of a porpoise in the British Encyclopaedia. We would jump like the Flying Porpoise over and over again, and always ended up tangling our arms and legs together and laughing until we got the hiccups. We hadn't done the Flying Porpoise properly since we'd been in foster homes.

We did try it once, on the bed in Youngy's house. That was a mistake. She said we'd broken the bedsprings, so she walloped our thighs until her hand stung.

I cried but Viv didn't. She had always been the brave one.

I missed her so much and longed to see her. I felt lost without her.

CHAPTER 14
RESULTS OF RULES

When I look back on the over two years I spent at the Girls School while I lived with the Downeys, I would like to tell of times that were enjoyable, times that imprinted a longing for learning. But I'm hard-pressed to find much that remains uncontaminated by rules and restrictions. I can recall but one teacher, Miss Eliason, a gentlewoman who taught art. She would bring her own books to tell us about painters and their techniques and show the paintings on an epidiascope. Some people called it a magic lantern, but she taught us its proper name. The epidiascope was a huge, cumbersome piece of equipment that projected images onto a much larger screen. Miss Eliason needed three girls to help her lift it onto a table. Everyone wanted to be chosen to help. The table wobbled, and I was sure that one day the glass plate or the large convex lens would tumble to the floor. But it never did during the two and a half years I was at the Girls School. Miss Eliason was popular and let us laugh and talk in class. I expect that the headmistress had given her the wobbly table hoping it wouldn't hold the epidiascope. That it might even fall. I'll bet the headmistress realized there was too much laughter in her classes. Laughter was frowned upon. "Do not laugh" was an unwritten rule at the Girls School.

Miss Eliason was unique. The rest of the teachers remain face-less to me, save for the one who was in charge, Miss Lamdon. She was the headmistress of the Girls School. She was a short, stout, fearsome battle-axe, of whom most of us were terrified. Viv, who had entered the school two years before me, had been expelled by Miss Lamdon. Viv's note "Miss B. is a boring bitch" was a most unladylike comment. To be a lady was an important task that the teachers at the Girls School tried to impart.

Except for the note, I thought Viv would have been a good candidate for ladylikeness. She always looked as though she came from a bandbox—not a hair out of place; the pleats in her gymslip were knifelike; her tie and white shirt were spotless; and the seam up the back of her stocking was as straight as a die. None of these qualities were sufficient to forgive the heinous crime of the passed note.

The Girls School was in a town fifteen miles from the Downey home. Dee and Aunty Downey were proud that I, their foster-child, was going to the Girls School. It was a respected school, and hardly anyone from the town passed the entrance exam. Taking an examination, one that decided your future, when you were eleven worried me. I didn't know what I wanted to be when I grew up, even though that seemed to be a popular question that the teachers asked.

I wasn't quite eleven when the teacher in the village school said, "There's a war on, so they're making an exception. You're going to be allowed to take a short version of the entrance exam." The exam was minimal—my teacher took me into the nurse's office and asked me some easy questions.

I was bowled over a week later when she said I was the only one from my school who passed and I would be going to the Girls School in September. I hoped I would make friends.

I was soon to find out.

It was the first day of school, and I was standing at the bus stop near the Downeys. I was a small girl, with reddish hair that almost reached my shoulders. Near me stood a tall girl with black hair that fell over her eyes. We saw we had the same school badge on our blazers. We smiled at each other and gradually starting exchanging bits and pieces of ourselves. Her name was Marjorie Land, and we discovered we were both evacuees from London. That fact made us feel like friends almost at once. Her mother was also an evacuee. A grownup one.

When I first met Mrs. Land, I asked her if her husband minded her being away with Marjorie, or if he'd rather she was with him in London. The minute I asked that, I wanted the ground to swallow me up.

Their answers came simultaneously: "My father's dead." "I'm a widow."

My gaffe cleared the way for us to be honest, like true friends. Marjorie and I would confide in each other and tell each other almost everything. Marjorie's mother worked at a war job in a factory near the town. We weren't supposed to know its whereabouts, but we did.

One day, months later when we were firm friends, we cycled there to see what it was like. On top of its high walls were rolls and rolls of barbed wire. It looked vicious.

A man in a dark-brown uniform had a rifle slung over his shoulder. He was pacing up and down. He called, "Hey, you two."

We cycled away as quickly as we could. We never went near there again.

I tried not to be jealous that Marjorie's mum was in town and mine had to stay in London; it didn't always work. Marjorie was kind and generous, and she would put her arm around me if she thought I needed it. I hadn't realized it then, but later two teachers told me that I had a tendency to over-emotionalize. I supposed that went hand in hand with being dramatic, but except for the play where I had the opportunity to recite poetry, I had little chance to display emotion at the Girls School.

The bus we travelled on to and from school was a double-decker. Its outsides were camouflaged black, yellow, and khaki, and the windows were painted black. There was a school prefect on every bus, coming and going. There were different prefects every week, but all of them said the same things:

"No talking."

"I can see you."

"You'll get a detention."

"This is your last chance."

The first time I heard the prefect say that, I felt mad. It was so unfair. Fifteen miles of sealed lips. It was like the worst foster home all over again. I wished I could say something clever, but I knew enough to keep my mouth shut. Later, Marjorie and I laughed at the school's silly rules.

We soon found out there were many more rules that we would have to try to understand and accept.

When we arrived at the bus terminus, the prefects on our bus told us to follow them: "It takes ten minutes, so don't dawdle. You get a detention if you're late."

I'd read about detentions in schoolgirl books, but I'd never had one in real life. I hoped Girls School didn't use the strap. My hand started smarting even at the thought.

Marjorie laughed. "Don't worry; they only want us to hurry."

We both trotted along, trying to catch up with the nameless prefects.

The strap of the box that held my gas mask broke. It was hard holding it and my new satchel, crammed with my sandwiches, notebook, and new unsharpened pencils as well as my plimsolls. Girls School had sent a list of supplies that were essential. They weren't easy to find. None of the shops in the High Street had any of them.

The worst was the school clothing list. I counted the items and worked out that it would take a year's clothing coupons. I knew I would be given a few more clothes coupons when I reached fourteen, but that was a long way off. The Girls School must have thought we were millionaires. The costs were exorbitant. Here is what they required:

- white plimsolls for physical training
- six pairs of white ankle socks
- four white shirts
- four pairs of brown lisle stockings
- two navy pleated gym-slips
- one navy worsted blazer
- two neckties with red, yellow, and black stripes
- four pairs of navy knickers
- one navy woollen cardigan
- one navy sleeveless pullover
- one black velour hat
- six short, close-fitting jackets (spencers)

Luckily Mum was clever. She wrote from London to a group of ladies who helped the families who didn't have enough money. They found a second-hand uniform, and Mum sewed badges on the blazer and seams on the gymslip. When she had finished, the group of ladies congratulated her on her sewing skills. The clothes looked like real Girls School uniforms. Grandpa treated Mum to a Green Line bus ticket so she could help me get fitted out. When I tried on the bits and pieces of the uniform, especially the hat, we laughed so hard that I almost wet the navy knickers.

"You look like a female version of Charlie Chaplin."

Mum smiled at the thought of Charlie. She loved his antics, especially in his silent movies. As for the spencers—what on earth was a spencer? Had the teachers made a mistake? I thought six spencers were probably six suspenders—those rubber buttons that stop your stockings from slipping down.

Marjorie solved the mystery. "My mother told me the proper name is singlet, and the only difference is that singlets are sleeveless but spencers have short or long sleeves."

I was shivering with cold already, and the thought of being without sleeves was unappealing.

There were hundreds of girls in the large assembly hall and we all looked alike—navy and white, with some coloured strips and stripes. The noise of the talking was like Uncle Cann's aviary, only ten times louder. The chattering ceased immediately when the sharp shrill of a whistle echoed throughout the hall. You could have heard a penny drop. The girls stood to attention and with small steps shuffled quickly into rows. Forty students lined up in each row.

I thought they must have been practicing for the women's army or cadets, because they clicked their heels together and turned their heads to see that the line was straight. There were about fifty of us who were new. We didn't know we were supposed to shuffle. The prefect in charge of us pushed us into rows, whispering, "After the announcements and the Lord's Prayer, follow us and we'll find which forms you're in."

As soon as she said "Lord's Prayer," I knew I would pretend. At the town's Baptist and Methodist churches I went to, I pretended every Sunday and was never discovered. I hoped I wouldn't be caught here. The girl in front of me was tall, so perhaps the teachers wouldn't notice me. How wrong I was.

The prayer began, and my arm was yanked by a thin teacher with a grey bun and wire spectacles. She pulled me to the side of the hall. "Every Christian girl says the Lord's Prayer. You may be new, but you're not exempt."

"But I'm not Chrithtian," I didn't mispronounce Christian purposely. I was nervous. It came out of my mouth like a giant lisp. The girls near us were bending their heads to listen. She glared at them. Not one laughed. She pushed me back in line and said she'd deal with me later. She fixed her eyes on me. Her look was poisonous.

My first day and I was in trouble.

The girls were racing through the Lord's Prayer and had reached "Forgive us our trespasses as we …" I knew the prayer by heart and mouthed the words to the teacher's satisfaction.

Her poisonous darts diminished.

The assembly finished and most of the girls disappeared. We new pupils were unsure what to do or where to go but tried to look eager.

My face stiffened as I stretched my lips into a false smile.

"You won't look so smarmy when you see the class lists. You'll probably be in the class for cretins." The voice came from a girl in the next row. You could tell she was powerful and had many friends. They gathered round her, holding each others' hands and brushing specks of dirt from their uniforms. They giggled at every remark. One of them pinched her nose with her thumb and finger and glared at me. I hoped I didn't smell. Marjorie had whispered that I looked shipshape in my almost-new uniform. I so badly wanted Marjorie to be on the same class list as me.

"The class lists for the first-form pupils are on this wall. There are four first forms. Find your names and move quickly to the room. The prefects will show you the way."

Five prefects stood in front of five lists. Why five lists? I wondered. She said four first forms. I didn't think they made mistakes in this school. I'd been in Girls School three-quarters of an hour and did not feel like schoolgirls in story books did. Those girls had fun. They always had escapades. Nothing had been fun here so far.

We looked on the list for form 1A. My name wasn't on it, nor was Marjorie's. We went to the list for form 1B. Neither of us was on that list. We looked on the one that had form 1C typed above it in red, and Marjorie's name was there. Mine was not. My lips trembled.

"At least we can write notes to each other on the bus. By the end of the year we'll have enough for a book. Don't look so serious. We can tell each other everything that's happened during the day." I knew she was trying to cheer me up, so I smiled a watery smile as she walked away with the 1C prefect. When I couldn't find my name in form 1D, I thought perhaps I'd missed it. Perhaps it was on the lists for 1A or 1B.

The tallest prefect called, "Come and look at this list. You're probably on this one. What's your name?"

I looked. The printing on the heading was larger and darker. "Yes. There you are. These other girls are with you."

I might have guessed. It was that unkind crew who thought I was a cretin.

"You're all in upper II parallel Y. Lucky things. You'll get the red-glove treatment."

What a name. What did it mean? What were the "red gloves," and why would we get the treatment?

I soon found out.

We'd scored top marks on our exam. Our teachers told us that we were clever and would move on quickly. "If you girls live up to your promise, you'll be in IV special next year. Three academic years in two. Work hard and do your best."

They made sure we knew the word accelerate. That's what we were—an accelerated group.

The two and a half years as a pupil at the Girls School was like an endless queue: waiting for school lunches, waiting for teachers to begin lessons, waiting for the four o'clock bell, and waiting for even one girl in the class to be friendly.

For me it felt more "un-accelerated."

The girl who was voted class president in upper II parallel Y called me "smelly evacuee" under her breath. Her friends smirked.

The teacher reminded us not to tell tales: "No tittle-tattling. Ladies keep silent about things that trouble them."

I sealed my lips, but my heart felt like stone.

On evenings and weekends, all I could dream about was going home, and not going to the Girls School. I always felt hungry: hungry for Mum, Dad, and Viv; hungry for my own street and my own school; and hungry for my London friends. I didn't know where some of them were. The high school near where I lived had been badly bombed and was being rebuilt. When I would be able to return, I knew finding my friends would be difficult.

Chemistry wasn't taught in my primary school. I had never seen a chemistry laboratory before. You had to wear a lab coat. If your hair was long it had to be pinned and then tied back. Even girls with pigtails had to bend them up and tie them together. You stood at long benches that had small square sinks and gas taps for the Bunsen burners; the way they were arranged was called stations, and at those stations we did experiments. We had a list of experiments we had to complete perfectly to get a good mark. We had to write every step we took in our science logbook. It wasn't easy, but it was exciting most of the time, except when the teacher was afraid we were going spill HCL (hydrogen chloride) or H2SO4 (sulphuric acid). When that happened, her face turned pillar-box red, and she spluttered her anger on our tunics. I was beginning to enjoy learning how to use a pipette and a burette. I also knew how to pronounce their names.

The teacher who taught us French had lived in Paris before the war. She was originally from Tours, and she said her Touraine accent was highly considered. French, art, and English literature became my favourite classes, made my days feel lighter and sunnier. Math did not. Geography and chemistry eventually became favourites.

The classes were passable, but the students were impossible. I couldn't break through their dislike of evacuees from London and their dislike of Jewish people. At every opportunity they said mean, unkind things. At least they didn't call me Kikey. My father had been called that when he was in school. I think the girls in up-per II parallel Y used me as a scapegoat, someone they could get into trouble. I was tripped going to my desk. I was blamed if ink was spilt on their pages. My schoolbooks disappeared, and I was never allowed to join their games, nor was I invited to their homes.

There was a loneliness to being different. It only got worse when a girl, a refugee from Hungary, arrived and joined our class. Her father had been killed by the Germans, but she and her mother had escaped to England. She and I were the only Jews in the school.

In her first Latin class, she was asked if she knew what *Di Mortuis Nil Nisi Bonum* meant. She translated it correctly: "Don't speak ill of the dead." As she did so, she put the lid of her desk up to hide her tears. I went over to comfort her and put my arms around her.

The teacher was very cross. "Get back to your desk immedi-ately, Joy!"

The rest of the class smirked, and the girls laughed at us and said, "See! Jews stick together."

I stopped caring. I had my friend, Marjorie, and we wrote notes to each other on the school bus daily. We thumbed our noses at the whole school and at the school motto. We had to learn to let it roll off our tongues in perfect Latin: "*Ubi semen ibi meses*—Where there is seed, there shall the harvest be."

When I was in IV special, the meaning of the motto became clear. Seven of the sixth-form girls were expelled. All were preg-nant. All had been dilly-dallying with soldiers. I didn't understand the implications then, but I felt the high level of excitement, shock, and judgment in IV special as the girls gossiped. Not one teacher told us what had happened.

One item on the school clothing list that was impossible to find was the leather purse. In it we were allowed to keep only our bus tickets, our lunch money, and our war-time ID card. That was all. Our cotton handkerchief's home was in our tunic's pocket, clev-erly hidden in the fold of a pleat. The leather purse had to be worn slung diagonally, from our right shoulder to our left side. It was hard to open if you were left-handed. I was glad I wasn't. Some of the girls in my class had breasts. I didn't. They would pull the thin leather strap as tight as they could to make their breasts stick out. I was jealous. I pulled my purse tightly, but it didn't make any difference. At night, when I undressed, I would look at my nothing breasts and willed them to grow. They looked like tiny, pale, pink buds. I thought I was deformed.

One Monday morning, before our maths class, we were told to go to the science lab. "Strip to your knickers. The doctor's here. You're going to have a medical exam. It's compulsory. Leave your shirts and tunics on the last three benches and wait outside the door." We shivered in the queue. I had goose bumps all over. The Girls School was always cold. Coal was rationed, and the school was heated for only one hour every day. It was a long wait in the freezing corridor. The lab door kept opening and shutting, opening and shutting. The school nurse appeared and disappeared, appeared and disappeared like the cuckoo in a cuckoo clock. She shouted our names, but I didn't see any of the girls come out again after they'd gone in. I supposed there was another door that led to another corridor.

Suddenly it was my turn. The door opened, and she shouted my name. I wasn't deaf and gave her a funny look as she put her freezing cold hands on my bare back.

"Hurry along, young woman. The doctor's a busy man. He hasn't got time for stragglers. Pick your feet up."

Why did they always harp on my feet? I wondered. I wasn't pin-toed. My ankles were weak and often gave way under me, but I was trying to strengthen them, and Marjorie's mum taught me some exercises that she said would help. I hoped the doctor wasn't going to touch my feet. I was ticklish.

We both walked to the end of the lab. The doctor was standing in the science teachers' room that separated two labs. He wore a doctor's white coat with buttons that looked as though they were about to burst. A stethoscope hung around his neck and bopped onto the file of papers he was holding. "Nurse. This one's birthday's on the second. Yes? I see she's from London. Born there. Hmm. Parents Jewish. Hmm. Nurse. Take these papers to the school office. Quickly now. Go."

There were beads of perspiration on his nose and on the top of his thin black moustache as he pulled on the elastic of my navy knickers and forced his way between my legs with his clenched fist. "No hair there yet. Shut your mouth. You'll like it one day. You Jews are all different up there."

My open mouth had let out only a squeak.

It had all happened quickly.

He then pinched my little pink buds and pulled on them.

I didn't know where I was hurting more, above or below.

And then it was over.

He heard the nurse coming and pushed me out another door. It slammed behind me. My legs felt shaky.

A teacher saw me in the hallway and said sharply, "What are you doing in the corridor? Back to your class."

She hadn't given me time to answer. I wasn't sure I'd know what to say. I didn't want to tell anyone. Not even Marjorie. Had he done that to all the girls in upper II parallel Y? Was it part of the medical exam? Was it part of growing up?

That night, alone in my triangle room, I undressed. I tried to see if my body looked different. It felt different. My breasts looked redder. There was a stain in my knickers. Perhaps I hadn't wiped myself properly.

"Good night," called Aunty Downey. "Are you ready?" I wished I could confide in her.

Perhaps I could tell Viv when I saw her.

But I never did.

Several days later, Aunty D. told me how proud she was. "Your teacher says you're smart. She likes your spark." I hadn't told Dee or Aunty Downey that I was in a poetry recital at school until it was too late for them to attend. I promised to tell them how the evening went.

I was on stage. I could see nothing in front of me and nothing below me, yet I knew the Assembly Hall was jammed. Crammed full. They were mostly women and young children, and all were coming to see us act. Earlier, I had peeked through the stage curtain, but one of the mothers who was helping pulled me back onto the stage and made sure my toes were on the chalk line. That was the marker for me. I had to start there and then move forward to the very front of the stage. I didn't like that mother. Her voice scratched, and her nails dug into my arm.

I stuck out my tongue at her back. The mothers were so bossy backstage.

I knew that most of the girls' fathers were in the armed forces. Nobody was supposed to know where their dads were posted but rumours crept out:

"My dad's in the desert. Don't tell anyone!"

"My uncle's ship is in the ocean, but I can't remember its name. It's a big one."

I wasn't sure if she meant the ocean or the ship. I wouldn't have forgotten the name of the ocean. Geography was my best subject.

Earlier in the evening, a girl boasted, "Well, my father's a major in the Welsh guards, and my mother says he spends most of his time drinking in the officers' mess."

In his weekly letter, Dad wrote about cousin Juhan, who was stationed in Yorkshire. Dad said, "Traipsing across the moors is not my idea of war."

I had seen a few old men in the audience, and I was glad they didn't have to traipse anywhere. And I was glad that some men would see the acting. I was happy my own father was too old to be called up. I wished my very own family was in the audience. This was my first ever acting on a big stage in a high school production, and I wanted someone there to be proud of me. The smell of the many hundreds out front sitting in damp clothes sodden from the day's downpour made my nose twitch. I hoped I wasn't going to sneeze.

I opened the production. The curtains swung back, and I strode forward to the second chalk marker. The glare of the stage footlights blinded me, and for one awful moment I forgot my lines. I heard a whisper from the mother who had hurt my arm: "Whither …," and away I went: "Whither, O splendid ship, thy white sails crowding, leaning across the bosom of the urgent West."

I accompanied my poetic delivery with grandiose gestures—which I realize now would be laughed to scorn but then were accepted and even admired as being in the great acting tradition. Mum used to tell me about the famous Victorian actor and actress Henry Irving and Ellen Terry. I wondered if Ellen Terry ever had to wear what I was wearing: three huge sheets wound around my middle and two draped on both shoulders. With sheets from top to bottom I looked like a bandaged accident. The bed sheets were hard to come by in wartime, yet the mothers had managed to scrounge and rescue, beg and borrow, and once, as one girl told us, steal.

Part of me wished they hadn't been so clever.

The silence in the hall gripped my throat. Not a cough, not a sneeze, not a titter of laughter. Then, as the last word of the poem slid from my tongue, there was a huge burst of applause.

A deep voice cried, "Bravo. Bravo, young 'un."

I bolted into the stage wings. I knew that underneath my powdered face I was blushing with shame for being a show-off. Shamed that the way I recited had embarrassed the rest of my class.

The day before, one of the girls had told me not to act with such a BBC voice. "Take that pebble out of your mouth and make some mistakes; you're only going to make us look bad. I think you're do-ing it on purpose. You don't usually speak like that."

But I didn't listen. I wanted to get back at them. They had been so mean to me.

Going home to the Downeys after my poetic performance, I practised how to describe the atmosphere of the evening. I antici-pated Betty's hugs. I wanted them to enjoy my retelling.

In my last few letters to Mum and Dad, I had expressed more strongly than ever how much I wanted to come home. I stressed to them that the bombing was just as bad in the country as it was in London, and we had spent most nights in the cramped bomb shelter in their cellar.

I had been so lucky being with Aunty Downey, Uncle Dee, and Betty. The two years away had been a big chunk of my life. I was proud that I had grown up. I had learned to deal with mean kids at school, and I had been a big sister to Betty. I knew it would be hard for them when I left, but I hoped that day would come soon.

CHAPTER 15

GOING-HOME DAY

A few weeks later, near the end of 1943, that day did come. I will always remember it.

I awoke with a start. My breath whistled a soft screech. My body wouldn't obey me. It was as if it didn't belong to me. It flooded over me like a huge wave. It wetted my nightie.

In a flash I knew what the flooding meant. It was the day. "Today's the day. The day it's going to happen. Today today today. It's going-home day. I'm going home home home. The happening is me."

It was dark outside. I strained my neck to peer out the window. No peek of light from any source outside, no beam from early workers' flashlights. Couldn't see the roof of the Panama Hat Factory. Couldn't know whether the night watchman had put the kettle on the hob.

"It must be early." I wanted the day to start. I wanted it to start so badly I felt infected. Like when I had scarlet fever. All my feelings hurt. My body hurt. Like those wireless waves on the crystal radio Dad made. When he put the two wire ends together, they sparked and sizzled. The sizzle went right through my body. Like it was doing now.

I didn't want to wake Dee. I couldn't stand it when he was grumpy; he stopped making jokes with me. He turned into a different bricklayer.

Aunty Downey said, "He'd be happy if you stayed here for good."

Dee never said good-bye if he could help it; when he had to say it, his face creased. Sort of crumpled. That was not going to happen to me. I would wave my good-byes. I practiced. It would make the light come quicker.

"Good-bye, saggy mattress. Good-bye, bed. Good-bye, triangle room. Good-bye, you old stinky loo. Good-bye to this foster home, this village, and that horrid, snobby high school and all its snotty pupils." My list was interrupted as the town clock struck the notes for the quarter.

"It must be quarter to six. It'll soon be light." My foot edged out of the covers. "Heck, I've wet the lino too." The clock struck again. Four long notes.

"Four o'clock. It's gotta be more. I want it to be more. Please be more."

But it wasn't.

And then it was.

My shoulders shook from side to side.

"Come on, sleepy Joy, it's nearly time for breakfast." Betty pulled the covers and snuck her legs in.

"Hey. It's soaking. Did you pee the bed? Even the lino's wet."

Inside my head, I sang, I don't care. I don't care. Outside, I sang to the tune of "Who Killed Cock Robin?" and "I'll mop it up. I'll mop it up."

Half giggling, half crying, Betty climbed in. She plonked herself on top of me.

"Not so tight, Betty. You're strangling me."

"Don't go, Joy," she sobbed and hiccupped. "Don't. I want you to stay. I want you to stay here forever. Don't you want to? Don't you like us? I thought you loved me. Who'll read to me? Who'll help me say my times tables?"

"Of course I like you. It's more than like, it's a sort of love. And I like and love your mum and dad too. And Uncle Teddy. There are different sorts of love. Our teacher said we'll understand when we grow up. You wait, and one day it'll happen. Dee will read to you and listen to your tables. Anyway, I have to go home. My mum and dad need me. And I need them," I whispered.

"Hey. Betsyboo. My neck's goin' to break in two. Awright. You can kiss me. Aargh! I think you've turned into Ma Cann's dog, Myrtle. Your kisses are as wet as hers. And I've told you how much I loved her."

A call came from below: "C'mon, you two. Up. Up. Breakfast's on the table."

I thought Aunty Downey's voice sounded different, and so did Betty.

"Mummy must have a cold or something. She stuffed five of Daddy's hankies in her pinny this morning."

I wondered whether my voice would come out like my everyday voice when I said my good-byes. I felt so different. I thought I was in a cloud. Will I have to come down to pretend I'm not happy at leaving? If I make a sad voice will they know I'm acting? Granny Shorter will. She knows me. This morning her voice sounds like a shuffling slipper. I hope she slept well last night.

"Look sharp and get down here, you two. Enough of that argy-bargy."

We grinned at each other and got dressed.

Aunty D. had made oatmeal with raisins and given me the cream from the top from the milk bottle on my helping. She brought out her best Sunday cups and saucers with the lilacs on them, her bone china wedding present bowls and plates, and put the tablecloth with lazy daisy stitches embroidered in pink onto the kitchen table. I looked at everything and wanted to say thank you but couldn't. I thought I might cry and laugh at the same time.

Viv used to say, "You've got the high-strikes again." She knew how to make me stop. She got my skin between her thumb and fingers and dug in hard. It worked every time.

I sucked in my breath and half closed my eyelids. I looked at Aunty D. Her eyes were red and puffy. My cheeks were wet and my lips tasted salty and I was all mixed up.

Does she think my tears are for her? They were only half for her. Doesn't she know I'm crying because I'm happy? I think my heart is going to burst. My mum is coming and I can't wait. When oh when will she be here?

Betty's eyes widened. "You're whispering, Joy, and your eyes look funny. Mummy asked you why you're not eating your porridge. Mine's almost gone. It's yummy."

I jumped when I heard the knocker.

"Open the door, Joy. I expect it's your mother …"

Betty's loud sobs drowned the rest of Aunty Downey's words. "I don't want her to go. I don't. Don't let her go. Don't go, Joy. Don't."

But I had already opened the door. I pulled my mum in and showed her what I had to carry: nearly three years of my life away from home stashed into my burlap haversack and a cotton pillowcase.

Mum and Aunty Downey were polite to each other.

"Please have a cuppa tea, Mrs. Abrahams, and a bite to eat. You must've left London at the crack of dawn."

"Thank you, Mrs. Downey, that's very kind. Yes. I am hungry. A slice of toast will go down well."

I wanted to laugh. It sounded as though they were acting in a play. Neither of them spoke like that in real life. Yet this was real life. This was the day. My day of going home.

I managed to eat my porridge. It didn't go down easily with Betty sniffling beside me.

Mum smiled at Aunty Downey. "I see you cook your porridge the true Scottish way. That's how I make mine. We have it winter and summer. When we can find it nowadays."

Aunty Downey smiled at Mum. She produced a large package from under the table. "This is for you to take to London. Uncle Teddy has a shop with his bakery, and he has things that are difficult to find, like these oats. There's some tea, too. Joy told me that you enjoy China tea. And Joy"—tears dropped on her cheeks—"there's a little parcel in there for you to remember us by."

"I won't ever forget you, or Dee and Betty." I quickly added Shorty's name. I felt generous. "I'll come back and see you when the war's over." I kissed Betty hard and licked her tears away.

CHAPTER 16

HOME ON GREEN LINE

Everything happened in a flurry. Our shopping bags, bulging with last-minute shove-ins, almost split their sides. "Like us," Mum said as we smiled at each other.

She cuddled me tightly as we sat on the bench waiting for the Green Line. Train tickets cost a lot of money, and going by train meant climbing up and down stairs to change to another train and crossing the train tracks by a bridge. It involved a lot of walking. It was too much for Mum and her swollen ankles. She lost her breath when she climbed steps, and if we had travelled by train she would have had to climb forty steps. Going on the Green Line was easier: not so much walking, and cheaper, less than half the price. Mum's smell made me feel light-headed. So often I had longed to inhale it, and now I was. It flooded over me in great waves. My breath became quicker and quicker. Deep inside I thought this moment was the happiest of my life.

I thought, I'll remember this forever.

Mum had a crackle in her voice. I hoped she didn't have a cold. She told me, as she pulled her hanky out of her pocket, that this was the only coach that went to our terminus. "We can get our local bus from there. If they're running. The driver on the coach I came on told me to come early so the queue wouldn't be too long. She said there might be no room because the roads were bad. This week the axles on two coaches had broken. Snapped like a wooden ruler. The driver said our roads are all beat up by the big army trucks."

Mum laughed, her crackled voice gone. "It's funny having lady drivers. Our upstairs flat woman can't stand it. But I like it. Lady drivers are careful—they don't take the bends so quickly."

I could have listened forever. I wanted her to go on talking and never stop. I was hungry: for her, for home, for Dad and Viv, for my bed, for our plates and cups, for our knives and forks, for our scullery, for our bathtub, and for her—my mum.

"Here, love, let me take them bags—I'll put 'em in the hold. Them others'll fit on the rack. Up you go, young 'un," and our conductor-bus driver helped me up onto the platform.

"Find yourself a seat that's not torn. If you can. No repairs done these days. Lucky enough to have this old bus. She's a relic from long before this war. She's going to be full you know, only two busses a day now, so there'll be lotsa stops on the way. There's some army boys goin' up to London. To see their girls, I bet." He winked at mum and me. I was hoping for a lady driver, but he sounded and acted jolly.

A voice behind us said icily, "Careful what you say, sir. Don't forget there's a war on."

"Can't never do that, missus, I've got two boys in the army."

The other passengers started clapping. An old woman near me wiped her eyes with a khaki hanky. "This was my son's," she whispered to Mum. "Dieppe. On the beachhead. With all his pals."

Mum blinked her tears away. My tears wouldn't stop. They fell for the lady whose son had been killed. My sorrow and happiness were mixed up together. Home. Home. I was going home.

I didn't care about food rationing. I didn't care about air raids. I was going to hold onto my mum and never let her go.

While these thoughts rushed through my mind, Mum placed her cheek on mine and smiled her wide, wide smile. I closed my eyes, and with a rumbling tummy I fell asleep.

I think I shouted. I woke my mum and the lady in the next seat.

"It's all right, little 'un," said a voice from the back. "S'only a dream."

"Where are we, Mum? Nearly there?"

"Nearly there, Joy. Not long now. Let's have a sandwich. It'll make the time pass quickly."

It was my favourite. Vorsht, with hot mustard, on rye bread and a sliced Bramley cooking apple that made my tongue tingle. Our family liked the taste of the tart cookers, and the greengrocer saved them for Mum when his supplies came in.

"You'll be able to carry the shopping for me and take the sheets to be washed. I know you'll be a big help," said Mum.

I didn't want to be a burden. Mum was working in the heart of London, and her journey on the crowded bus took forty-five minutes. Dad didn't have as far to go. He cycled. He called his bicycle "my old clunker." It did make clunky noises even before the war. He used to give me rides on the crossbar until Mum said it was too dangerous.

On the trip home, Mum told me I might find Dad different. He was often tired and irritable. She explained that he hated the place where he worked. One man there made hateful remarks about Jews every day, and it got on Dad's nerves.

Mum told me Dad was so upset by the name-calling that he decided to change his surname from Mark Abrahams to Mark Scott. "Your father thinks it's a good business name and sounds much less Jewish. And after the war, Scott and Scott Advertising will draw less attention from anti-Semites than Abrahams and Abrahams."

I wanted to keep my name. And I knew Viv would too. We liked being Joy and Viv Abrahams. "Dad can't make me change my name," I insisted.

Mum asked me to be patient with him. I thought I had learned a lot about patience in those foster homes, but I wasn't sure. "I'm growing up quickly, Mum. You'll see. I'm thirteen and a bit. I'll do my best."

The journey was over. We had managed with all our bits and pieces: my dear old haversack, Aunty Downey's parcel of presents, and Mum's carrier bag for the leftovers. I was sleepy, but when I saw the holes and gaps in the streets, my mouth dropped open. Some of those holes were near number 131, our house. The house next door-but-one was propped up by a tall triangle of timber; the inside looked like a skeleton. It was the Hawleys' house. Rose Hawley had been in Viv's class at school. I hoped they hadn't been home when the bomb fell.

The way Dad and Viv welcomed me helped me realize they had missed me as much as I had missed them. Viv was a good cook for a fifteen-year-old, and she knew that macaroni and cheese was my favourite. She baked it with a brown crusty top. It was delicious.

"Aunty Phyllis gave me six of her meat coupons, and the grocer's wife gave me an extra nob of cheese when I told him you were coming home."

Mum said it was hard to work out what to have for meals with the rationing and the coupons. "Your sister is a very good manager and arranger. I hope you'll take after her."

I didn't want to be an arranger. I preferred to read. I knew there was one thing I wouldn't make or eat: scrambled eggs from dried egg powder. They tasted like ground-up yellow chalk.

That night we had Viv's scrumptious cooking, and Dad and Mum brought me up-to-date with family news.

I learned Uncle Jack was in the army and was posted in the Orkneys. He called it the North Pole and wrote to his wife complaining about the freezing cold weather and boring days and nights. Aunty Netty was directed to look after babies in a nursery. She washed their soiled nappies daily, in cold water, and had chilblains on her eight fingers. She said the babies' crying got on her nerves. Dad told her that was because she'd never had children of her own. She said she didn't like children and had no intention of having a family. Cousin Derek, my favourite cousin, was in the Royal Air Force and was stationed abroad. He sent Mum a snapshot of himself and his friend in Africa. They were dressed in shorts and were standing in front of a hotel near a beach. The snapshot looked like the seaside in England; I wondered where the war was.

Dad said Tortoise had disappeared—that the bombs had probably scared him and he'd gone underground. He'd kept quiet about it. He'd hoped he'd reappear. Mum told us about our chickens. We now had a chicken coop and six laying Leghorns.

"It'll be your job to feed them, Joy, and look for the eggs."

We talked until our mouths were dry. Mum and Dad said they would do the washing-up and that Viv and I should go to bed, otherwise we'd never wake up. Before I went up the hallway, I opened the door to our back garden. It was pitch black. Quiet.

I whispered, "Tortoise. Where are you? Come back, Tortoise. Please come back."

CHAPTER 17
LUNCHING ON HISTORY

E arly in 1944 it felt that the war was never going to end. I was happy to be back in London. I had reconnected with friends who had been evacuated. I was adjusting to life at school and at home.

We didn't see much of our relatives during this time. Travelling around London was not easy, and most of the family were involved with the war effort.

One day, the postman pushed a large envelope through our letterbox. I was excited. I ran into Mum and Dad's bedroom and woke them. "Look, Mum, it's a posh invitation for Sabbath luncheon."

"You open it," said Dad. "Who's it from?"

"It's from Great-Aunt Henriette!"

"Hetty always makes a splendid table, so we'll put our *Shabbos* clothes on," Mum said, "but I don't need her looking down her nose at me, giving me that 'poor relation' sympathy look and a bag of cast-off clothes to take home."

Her angry tone surprised me. Mum rarely raised her voice. I enjoyed sorting through the bags of cast-offs that our relations sent. I liked trying on the posh clothes that smelled of lavender. But I didn't say anything. I didn't want Mum to be angry with me.

Mum replied to the invitation, saying we would be happy to come, but unfortunately, Viv was needed for work at her latest hair salon.

Aunty Hetty lived near Mill Lane with her husband, Joe. Uncle Joe was a bookie who spent most of his time at the greyhound races. Her three spinster sisters lived not too far away on Munster Road. Dad knew the bus route. It went up Shoot-Up Hill, followed by a ten-minute walk to Aunty Hetty's house.

Aunty Hetty had been a headmistress at a girl's school and was very strict.

"You'd better mind your p's and q's with Hetty, my girl," said my father. "She's a no-nonsense woman."

I believed he was a little afraid of her. He never teased her. I think he knew *he* was the one who had to mind his p's and q's. I didn't have to. She said I could call her Hetty. It felt a bit strange, but I did, and we talked about books and ideas. I was proud that she treated me like a grownup.

"Hetty is an educated woman. A woman before her time," my father confidently claimed of the relationship.

'Before her time' intrigued me. Was this what it looked like? Her raven-black hair was pulled back in a tight bun. Tiny pince-nez glasses perched on the end of her nose and were fastened to her chest with a small gold safety pin. She wore a corset that flattened her chest and hips. Its bones bulged, allowing a stripey pattern to show through her grey dress, and her body seemed bandaged like an Egyptian mummy. She never slouched.

The first thing she said to me was, "Hold your head up, girl. Don't jut your chin out. Keep your back straight. Put this book on your head and walk to the door."

Maybe walking with my chin in and my back straight would help me be a woman before my time.

I hadn't seen Aunty Hetty or her sisters and brothers since 1933, and I was very young then. I did remember them patting my cheeks and giggling. Dad and Mum wrote to them when we lived in the West Country, and I often sang their names and imagined them in a chorus line: Israel, Simeon, Raphael, Julian, Gabriel, Mimi, Lily, and Julie.

They were my father's oldest cousins, but Viv and I called them uncle and aunty.

"Hetty, leave the gal alone," Mimi, Julie, and Lily chorused. "She's probably hungry. We have to catch up on lost time and want to get to know her again."

I was excited to be with them in Aunt Hetty's parlour, with its huge, oblong mahogany dining table and enough seats for everyone. They were all there for lunch except Uncle Simeon. "He has a big meeting at his club," said Aunt Hetty.

When I looked at my three "spinster" aunts' clothes, I noticed how threadbare the fabric was. I was sure it bothered them. Before the war they had been quite fashionable, and now their clothes were worn and frayed.

Aunty Mimi was excitable and giggled more than her sisters. Her real name was Miriam, but she made everyone call her Mimi. My father, a dreadful tease, would burst into a fine operatic tenor as in "La Boheme" as he sung her name. "Mi-mi!" I knew he was making fun of her, but I was never quite sure why until that day I saw her at Hetty's house.

Her rib bones stuck out clearly from her thin body and were patterned across her chest like a ladder of sticks. They made the bones in her cheeks, those two little round balls, look as though they were waiting for a baseball strike. Her wig was unable to contain her white hair, which descended wispily. The wig was jet black and shiny, shiny like the piece of anthracite that Aunty Downey had pushed to the bottom of my Christmas stocking when I was her foster child. Mimi's voice intrigued me. It was squeaky, like a door hinge that hadn't been oiled, and breathless, as though she had sprinted a hundred yard race. Despite her squeaks and breathing, she sang almost non-stop, popular songs from the Music Halls: "When I'm Cleaning Windows," and "Harbour Lights."

Mimi was dressed in a pink skirt made of organdy. A see-through skirt. I could see her skinny legs and white smooth camiknicks. Below them, the small, round rubber button at the end of her suspender belt bulged from the top of her thigh. She wore a black blouse, tight-fitting, with ruffles at her neck and wrists. But the ruffles didn't hide the craggy wrinkles of her neck, and there was no protection to hide those on her face. The frightening thing to me, then, was her makeup. Eyebrows pencilled in heavy black, not where her thin eyebrows were faintly visible; these were scrawled in the middle of her forehead. They looked ferocious and emphasized the huge brown bags under her eyes—bags that suggested weeks of sleepless nights.

She sidled and sashayed close to my father: "Oh, Mark," her voice wheedled and caressed. "You're as handsome as ever. If you weren't my cuz', I'd jump right into bed with you."

"Mimi!" Hetty's voice warned. "None of that talk in front of Mark's daughter."

It felt as though she was stroking his cheek, and a lump stuck in my throat. I tried to cough it away. I felt sad. As I saw the way Mimi looked and how she flirted with my father and batted her eyelids at us all. It was as though she was standing there in her camiknicks. Stripped like an uncovered mattress. Nearly naked.

She bantered, "Sister, Mark knows I've loved him since he was in grey socks and short pants. I wouldn't rob the cradle even if I was tempted."

Uncle Joe's voice muttered from the corner of the large parlour, "A quarter of a century older than Mark. Might've posed problems."

Smothered titters and giggles softly filled the air as Mimi trilled, "When I grow too old to dream, I'll have you to remember."

I loved her singing and I loved that song. I clapped until my hands stung.

Mimi was a soprano and sang in the choir at the local *schul*—synagogue.

At the time, many people thought a choir in an orthodox synagogue should not be allowed. But it was in our synagogue.

Great-Aunt Hetty told me *schul* was the German word for school. "You can learn a lot about the history of our people if you study hard."

The choir was the *schul's* pride and joy. Probably some of the former rabbis were turning in their graves when they heard of the mixed choir, but Mimi said that the men and women stood and sang from opposite sides of the gallery. It's the same as they do in the main sanctuary.

"Men and boys, women and girls separate. They mustn't touch each other. It's not easy to get the four-part melodies when you're separated, and I like rubbing shoulders with the men."

She rolled her right shoulder and then her left, and I could see her tiny, pointy breasts. She looked frail and at the same time not frail, as though there was a thin wire pulling her straight in like a core—her centre of gravity.

I was nearly thirteen. Often I was confused about my feelings. I was unsure about families and grownup behaviour. Some days my stomach wouldn't stop churning. Now I was back with my family, and I was still trying to sort out God and Jews and war. I hadn't celebrated any Yom Tovs since before the war.

When I was evacuated, I never forgot I was Jewish, even though I went to church three times a day on Sunday for more than three years. Including school assemblies, I had recited the Lord's Prayer 223 times and knew every hymn in the hymnals. I had been to High Church, Methodist, Baptist, Episcopalian Congregational, and almost Seventh Day Adventist. I pretended to say "Jesus" and "Christ" in all those buildings and said my Hebrew prayers every night. "*Shema Yisroel Adonai Elohenu Adonai Echad*. Hear, O Israel, the Lord is our God, the Lord is One." I hoped God would understand that I had no choice. I hoped he would forgive me.

If there was a God.

"The war has made a big dent in our lives," Mimi declared.

The silence that followed felt like thunder. The "dent" she spoke about felt more like a volcanic eruption. Raging, raging. The previous week in *schul* we had said *Kaddish*, our memorial prayer, for our long-distance relatives who had died in Europe. I knew them all from a faded snapshot of a summer picnic taken in a field outside a small village near Lvov, Ukraine. They were smiling, so I expect they were happy, but I thought they would have been more relaxed if their clothes had been more casual. They, men and women, boys and girls, were buttoned and belted, beribboned with bows, and their feet were encased in black boots. I had breathed and fingered that photo every night during the war. I had rubbed their faces so much they were nearly blank. Dad hadn't told us what happened to them. He had heard from someone who had escaped from the Warsaw ghetto and had managed to get news to his family. We learned they had been taken to a gravel pit, shot, and shovelled in. When I heard that, I didn't want to grow up.

Perhaps Mimi had heard a different horrid story, and she flirted with men to prepare for any invasion. I couldn't puzzle it out. I realized I was too young to understand what went on between men and women, but I was old enough to realize that if you're touching someone all the time, you probably want to be touched back.

My father stuck out his lanky arm and said, "The list of our lost relatives and those of our friends is as long as my arm—and longer. And those were only the ones on my side."

He listed more and more names: the Dobnows and Greenbergs. My mother couldn't talk about it. I was glad she carried at least four or five of my father's white handkerchiefs in her black handbag because I was a big crier. I knew that if she started crying, so would I.

"I'm grateful that most of my side is Sephardic. Originally they came from Portugal and then escaped to Holland. But we've been in England hundreds of years. Look." She pointed to an enamelled turquoise pendant inscribed in silver:

"Lodge of Israel–1795"

There didn't seem to be one place we could go without being disliked because we were Jews. But here I felt safe in the hustle and bustle of setting food on the table. Aunties Mimi, Julie, and Lily chirped and twittered like their budgie, Shushi. They surrounded my mother and me.

I was hungry. I was looking forward to the food and eating with the shiny silver knives and forks. There were three different shapes of glasses and porcelain soup tureens with flowers painted all around the bulges. I didn't mind our not having the best sets of china, nor did I mind being poor. Well, not too much. I was beginning to understand what having possessions meant to families.

Earlier in the week, I had seen the look on the face of the girl I sat next to in school when she came to our cold, furniture-less dump of a flat in a rundown, bombed-out part of London. It was then I wished we had nice chairs to sit on. Her look had been full of disdain.

Aunt Hetty boasted about her home. "Those Edwardians knew their architecture. Look at my place. Solid, brick built. Strong pediments. Plaster pargeting from Georgian times on my high ceilings. And I'm having our three-piece in the parlour and the one in Joe's sitting room recovered. And the library repainted."

I hadn't realized Uncle Joe had his own sitting room. I wondered what he did in there.

He was eighty-eight, and Dad used to joke, "The only thing Joe reads are the bookies' tables. He's a dyed-in-the-wool gambler. He'd go to the greyhound races every day if his cranky legs didn't bother him. Hackney Wick Stadium used to be his home-away-from-home."

My voice rose high. "It's mean to make greyhounds chase a pretend hare."

"You're a hypocrite, young lady. You accepted the half-a-crown from his winnings that Joe slipped in your hand."

My father was right. I had. Half a crown went a long way when you didn't have much money.

Oh! How inviting the table looked.

Aunt Hetty's voice bellowed, "To the table. Let's eat," and she showed everyone their place.

"I've given you your great-great-aunt Julia's silver serviette ring, Joy." My eyes popped when she said, "Look at the engraving. It's the same as your initials. JRA. Her middle name was Raie, the same as your mother's. You'll have it when you're sixteen—for your trousseau."

"I'm not getting married, Hetty. I haven't met anyone I fancy," I joked.

"None of that smart talk, my gel," said Raphael. His voice surprised me. I hadn't heard him say a thing so far.

"Enough of this schmoozing," Gabriel moaned. "I'm starving. Let's eat, like Hetty said. The bourekas will be cold and the egg and lemon turbot will be warm. I loathe cold bourekas and lukewarm fish."

The table looked splendid. I could see Mum's eyes light up as she and Dad exchanged glances. He knew how much she missed her own parents. Her mother, my grandma Sarah, could cook anything. The family called her a real *balabusta*, which meant she was not only a good cook, she could make a home into a palace. They didn't have much money, but she could make something out of nothing.

We blessed the bread, washed our hands, and ate. And we ate. And we told stories. Julie, Mimi, and Lily told about their war lives in Scotland. Julian and Raphael told about their work in a factory that made aeroplane parts, and Gabriel told about his life as a special constable.

They asked me about my time in foster homes, but I wouldn't talk about it. I couldn't. I never wanted to talk about it again.

"You're home now, and that's all that counts." Mimi gave me a squeeze.

I felt full. Full of stories, full of food, and full of family. I think everyone felt the same. Uncle Joe had loosened his trouser belt two notches.

Aunt Hetty was wriggling in her corset. "These bones are killing me." I'd never heard her be so un-headmistress-like.

Aunty Julie undid the safety pin in her skirt fastening. A seamstress using a safety pin surprised me. And cousins Julian, Raphael, and Gabriel loosened up.

"Call us Jules, Raff, and Gabby—the Marx brothers of the family." Laughter bounced off the high ceiling.

After we had said our thank yous and kissed and hugged and been hugged and kissed, we walked to our flat four miles away. Uncle Joe had offered to pay for a taxi, but Mum said she liked walking and that the air would do us good. I knew she didn't like walking, and I wished she'd taken his offer. She always felt embarrassed when our relatives wanted to give us money.

The air was damp and cold, and I didn't think it would do me any good at all. We had to walk down Shoot-Up Hill. It was a long, long hill, and my mother's ankles hurt.

"Look," Dad said, "that's where they live—Mimi, Julie, and Lily." It didn't look nearly as posh as Aunt Hetty's house.

Dad continued. "They're only scraping a living with their dressmaking, and I know that Hetty and Simeon are paying the rent." His voice lowered. I tried hard to catch the words, but all I heard was "tipple" and "man-crazy."

I heard Mum's whisper. "Don't forget her fiancé, Henry, was killed in the Great War and that other man she went with drank like a fish."

I was glad we didn't drink. The man in the upstairs flat came home drunk most nights. It scared me. I'd lean against my bedroom door and pray he wouldn't try to push my bedroom door open. He never did. Just banged up the stairs and shouted at his wife.

⚊⟋ ⟋⚊

Three weeks after Aunt Hetty's lunch party, I was helping my mother sort the laundry in our scullery.

"Your father and I don't want you to be upset, but we want you to see this." She told me to go into the kitchen and placed a page from a newspaper in front of me.

"It's only the local *Gazette,* and we don't think it made the national papers—but it does have her name and address and details about her singing in the choir." Without looking, I knew. I went stiff and held my breath. What if she'd fallen down the stairs drunk and had broken her neck? I snapped out of those fears and read:

"Choir Member of Orthodox Synagogue Reveals All. Delivery Man Startled at What Appeared Before Him. 'Bare Naked She Was!' said Frank Bingham. 'Not the First Time,' said a Neighbour. 'Go Away, Please!'"

My eyes blurred and the lines ran into each other. This wasn't the Mimi who'd teased my father, who'd squeezed and hugged me, who'd planned to start sewing again. The man who'd written the exposé used words familiar yet unfamiliar, like "lecherous" and "soliciting." I hated him.

The next week we received a letter from Julie and Lily. The handwriting was wavery. Mimi had been taken to a mental institution.

"It's forty miles from London. She has to stay there for six months or longer. She hates it. She's allowed visitors once a week. Please visit, Mark and Raie. We know it's a long bus ride, but do visit. You have to be over sixteen to get in the gate."

I was glad I was under sixteen and would not be expected to go. I did not want to see Mimi caged. I wanted Mimi to be the Mimi of our family luncheon. I thought I would write a story about a caged budgerigar and send it to her. It wasn't that brilliant of a story, but as I pushed the envelope into the red pillar-box at the end of our road, her song rose to my lips: "When I grow too old to dream, I'll have you to remember."

CHAPTER 18

TENSIONS TALLIED

"War Still Raging in Europe" the headlines in the dailies screamed. "V-1s and V-2s Falling on London." The rockets were guided missiles; their dangers were scary. It was the fall of 1944.

"Call themselves newspapers, those dailies. They're rags, that's what they are," said Dad. "Fear-mongerers. It's bad enough to have these new kinds of bombs without those rags showing us the damage. The only decent papers are the *Times* and *Telegraph*."

At school we were getting fed up with the air-raid sirens wailing. The V-1s had started, and we hoped things at school would get better—but they didn't. We were right back at square one. To make up for it, whenever we could, we would sing, "Ere we go again, 'appy as can be, all good pals and jolly good company." When we reached the "La di dah di dah" bit, our voices dripped with sarcasm. It was a way to make up for some of the lousy news.

Yvonne Hoskins, a lanky, quiet girl in our class who we all claimed as a friend, was homeless. Her house had been hit. Luckily, she and her seven brothers managed to get out before they were buried under the bricks, but the chimney had fallen on her mother and her back was broken. She couldn't move her legs. A neighbour took care of Yvonne's baby sister during the day, but after school, when she got to the homeless shelter, Yvonne had to cook supper and help her brothers with their homework, feed the baby, and then do her own. We didn't know how we could help. We didn't know what to do. We didn't know what to say. None of us had room to sleep the Hoskins in our homes. The shelter was an hour and a half's ride from our school, and the busses were still unreliable.

"We're fine, thank you. The shelter people said they'd find somewhere for us soon. Please pray for my mother. I take my brothers to Mass most mornings, and I'm sure God will hear our prayers." She spoke with such conviction. I didn't feel the same way. God hadn't listened to many of my prayers. I wanted him to change my body. Especially the front of my ankles and the parts of me that Sis and Dad called chubby. When I looked in the mirror I remained the same, even when I had kneeled and prayed for half an hour.

When my knees couldn't bear my weight any longer I got up. Sis mocked me: "Jews don't pray on their knees."

"Well I do. Don't you remember Aunty Bosworth told us we could and that God wouldn't mind?"

Sis rolled her eyes. "Now we're living back with Mum and Dad. We have to pray how they do. You watch them and see how they do it when we go to synagogue. At the Liberal Synagogue, at least we can sit together. Watch Dad closely, especially when he's moving his lips."

I did try to pray at the synagogue, but it didn't work. I wondered if it was because I didn't have a *tallis*—a prayer shawl. All my praying hadn't helped me to become better at physical training. However, I became strong in history, especially when I was asked to present an argument from a different point of view.

Miss Freehill, our history teacher, was a kind gentlewoman. She was never sarcastic to us girls. She was very knowledgeable about European, Russian, and American history.

When she would ask you to approach her desk, she would say, "Speak up, I'm a little hard of hearing, my dears."

There was but one disadvantage. Miss Freehill had a severe case of halitosis. It was impossible for most of us to prevent her extremely bad breath from reaching our nostrils.

Despite that disadvantage, we would have interesting discussions about the history and place of religion in the world.

"Some of my best friends are Jewish," she once confided to me on a bus ride home, "and for you, Joy, I am sure the discussions you and your family have during your meals add to your general knowledge. I will never forget the time I was invited for a Sabbath meal; the Jewish traditions are so evocative, it made me think of wanting to change my own."

A person of an entirely opposite nature was our very strict physical training teacher. Most of our class was afraid of her. She scared me stiff. Her name was Miss Lawrence, and she never let us forget she had been at Roedean, a famous boarding school for girls. Her favourite boast was that she and the great niece of the Tsar of Russia used to play tennis together. Some of the girls were impressed. Not me. I had read what the Tsar had done to his poor subjects. I thought Miss Lawrence would have fit in with the Tsar.

We wondered how old Miss Lawrence was; perhaps nearly seventy. Her hair was white and her face was pale and she never wore lipstick. We were probably wrong.

"She can't be that old," said our class prefect, Sylvia. "Old people don't wear kilts."

Miss Lawrence's kilt swung from side to side when she strode down the corridor. You could hear *swish, swish* even if you were round the corner. Aileen was born in Aberdeen. She knew a lot about kilts and Scotland. She said the tartan was from the Campbell clan.

In our bombed-out playground we used to sing, "The Campbells are coming. Hurrah. Hurrah."

We never sang it when Miss Lawrence was on corridor or playground duty.

All the teachers had favourites. Miss Lawrence had three in our class. They were allowed to be leaders, fetch equipment, and choose the teams in every class. In two whole years, I was never chosen to be a leader.

Dad taught us to bowl, and I was chosen for the first rounders and first tennis teams.

My bowling was accurate, very fast, and my throws from the deep field hit their mark. My tennis serves were fierce.

Miss Lawrence was angry when I missed a serve. "If you weren't such a good thrower and server, you'd be off my first team one, two, three. More brains and less brawn, young woman." If I didn't have brawn, how could I have played as well as I did? I hated her mean talk.

That summer Miss Lawrence wrote the brain-brawn statement on my report card. Perhaps she thought it was a clever observation, and perhaps it was, but I was mortified.

The worst thing for me was when I had to kneel on my knees and sit back on my heels.

Miss Lawrence spoke loudly and icily: "One member of this class is obviously not listening. She seems determined to kneel forward, not sit back on her heels as she was politely asked to do."

All heads would turn to discover the culprit. Of course it was me. I couldn't do it. The pain was excruciating. I wished I had a knife to cut my tendons so my ankles could point properly. I wished I could sit back on my heels, and Miss Lawrence wouldn't have to come and push my head down to make my tendons work.

"You're not trying, girl. Push harder. Use your energy." She sounded scornful as her cold hand pushed my head hard and harder. She hurt my head, my neck, my back, and my ankles.

"She doesn't like you," Jean Proudfoot said to me. "She doesn't like any of you Jews. Listen, and you'll hear how her voice changes when she speaks to you. My uncle doesn't like you Jews either. He says you're money-grubbers."

I felt a blocking noise inside my head, and my ears refused to listen to her hateful words. Would this name-calling ever cease? Would I ever be able to be "one of the crowd" and not be singled out as "that Jew kid"?

I wanted to scrawl on the wall: "Remember! Jews have feelings!"

CHAPTER 19
BROAD BEAMS RELEASE

My physical training life changed when I joined the gym club. The club had nothing to do with Miss Lawrence or the Girls School. It was quite separate. Two girls played a big part in helping me become a member because you weren't allowed to join unless you were voted in. Every member of the club had a vote, and the committee made up of parents had the final say. Paula Smith and Monica Evans voted me in. They belonged before the war, and their parents helped with the displays and the accounts and their votes counted.

Paula and Monica assured me the two ladies who owned the club were kind and encouraging, even to girls like me who couldn't point their toes properly. "Not everyone is a good gymnast. The owners, Dot and Merry, believe we should all have a chance. They make it fun. They giggle with us. They'll laugh at your funny feet. You'll see."

I wasn't sure I wanted to be laughed at. When I was teased I usually felt cross, but the sound of their names, "Dot and Merry," made me smile, and I couldn't wait to start.

When I asked Mum and Dad, they said they thought they could afford the monthly bill.

"Yes. You can go, but you must go with someone. It's quite a long way to go in the dark alone, and I don't want to worry," Mum said anxiously.

"Perhaps it'll work some of that puppy-fat off," Dad joked.

Viv wasn't home, so I didn't have to listen to her comments about my figure. She was still as thin as a needle. She looked good in whatever she wore. I was jealous of her figure and her good looks, but sometimes it didn't matter and my jealous feelings vanished into thin air when we played and sang together. We sang softly every night after we were supposed to not talk anymore. We stood up for each other when Dad got too cross and bad-tempered.

There was one big roadblock to joining the gym club. Dot and Merry's gym club met on Friday evenings. Friday evening was our *Shabbos*—the night we lit two tall candles, blessed the wine and challah, the plaited bread, and had a special Sabbath meal. It's true that the war had changed the way we celebrated *Shabbos*—Dad's and Mum's war work, late shifts, and bus delays all affected *Shabbos*. Often they didn't get home until very late. Viv and I would start the dinner and lay the table with our *Shabbos* cutlery and dishes, but then we got fed up with waiting. We were hungry, and the food was getting overcooked.

"Everything's spoiling," Viv moaned. "I promised to go to Wingate with Elsie, and if they don't come home soon, I'm leaving."

We were lucky. As she said that, in they both came. They looked tired, but I knew I was going to get an answer this *Shabbos*. Mum and Dad had been talking and had come up with a way to remove the roadblock.

"It's true," said Dad, "that we aren't as observant as we were before the war, but it doesn't mean we can't be good Jews and try to follow the Ten Commandments. Mum and I are all in on Fridays and you two are full of energy. We want you both to know more about your history and religion, and it's important to learn Hebrew and read the prayers. So." Here he paused for a long time. "If you both attend Sunday school at the synagogue every week, you, Viv, can go out with Elsie on Fridays, and you, Joy, can go on Fridays to Dot and Merry's."

We rushed and hugged Dad and Mum and squealed with happiness.

"At last," I breathed softly, "at last, at last."

Dad had the last word. "Who knows? We may not recognize you by Rosh Hashanah."

Rosh Hashanah, the Jewish New Year, was a good six months away.

"And who knows?" I said to myself. "I could be half a stone lighter by then. Maybe Dad *is* a prophet."

Pat North and I cycled to gym club every Friday. She lived up the road and round the corner from our flat, but she didn't mind calling for me, even if it did mean backtracking.

Mum was happy when Pat banged on the side door of our downstairs flat.

"She's a polite girl. I think that private school her father sends her to teaches her good manners. And she's tall and strong, so I don't worry any more about you both riding home in the dark."

"Oh, Mum. Don't be a worrywart. We won't get into any trouble."

I began to love Friday evenings and the gym club. With two owners like Dot and Merry, who wouldn't? They were warm and bubbly and never spoke unkindly, not even to girls like me who couldn't do handstands or back bends. I still had trouble pointing my toes, and I couldn't vault the pummel horse for love or money.

Dot always yelled enthusiastically, "Good try, Joy. You'll clear it next time."

"Jump harder on the springboard," Merry said. "That'll help you get your legs up and over."

Monica's mother gave me a white gym tunic that was too tight under the armpits for Monica. We had to wear the tunics when we performed for our parents. The tunics were split on each side up to our waists, as there had to be room for our legs to jump over the horses. The flaps fell over our faces when we did handstands. It was hard not to giggle. My favourite gym activity was pyramids.

"You've a good strong beam." Dot said. "You can be on the bottom with Monica, Joan, and Pat." I didn't realize that beam meant backside, but when I looked over I saw that all four of us had wide backs and beams. Six other girls climbed onto our backs and more girls climbed onto their shoulders and performed various pyramid poses. Audiences cheered loudly whenever we posed. I felt proud at having a beam that was appreciated.

Dot and Merry made a huge decision. They would take us gym clubbers camping, as many of us who wanted to go. Every weekend. We couldn't believe our luck. They knew a farmer who had a big field forty miles from London. He said we could camp on his field every weekend. For free. All we had to do was write our names on the chalkboard at the back of the gym and bring a few rations and the signed permission from our parents.

When they told us, we sang in chorus to the tune of Beethoven's Fifth "V for Victory" phrase. "No more Vee-ones. No more Vee-twos." That had helped us stay positive during some of the war's dark days. We used to sing it at the Downeys. The words were slightly different: "No more big bombs. No more big bombs." The tune was the same. I was glad we were using it again.

When the sirens were not screaming, we had peaceful sleeps. It looked like my school life and my air-raid life had changed since I joined the gym club. Miss Lawrence's remarks and pushes on my head didn't make me cringe anymore, and I felt glad that I would have the chance to sleep in a tent. I hadn't slept in one since before the war. I thought our being in an open field would make it easier to see if a missile was coming our way.

We went to gym on Friday nights as usual, and those of us who were going camping concentrated very hard and performed our very best. We didn't want to disappoint Dot or Merry when they were doing so much for us. We went home exhausted. Dot and Merry were ready to leave at eight in the morning on Saturdays. We arrived on time and waited at the gym. No one wanted to miss one second of the trip. We made sure we had completed our homework, but if we were lucky, we persuaded our teachers not to give us any. Our teachers seemed tired and worried about things outside school, so it wasn't hard to get them to ease up on the homework.

Some of the fifteen- and sixteen-year-old gym-clubbers had jobs. Daphne worked in a factory, and Eileen worked in a camera shop. They had to work on Saturdays and could never have it off. Monica and I were surprised by how many of the clubbers' parents had refused to sign the permission form.

"Perhaps they've been evacuated long enough," Monica said. "It's hard convincing my father to let me come." I knew what she meant. Her father had been wounded at Rouen and was discharged from the army. When I went into their kitchen, he would tell Monica off for not having folded her clothes or done the shopping. He was very strict. One day I thought he was going to hit her with his walking sticks.

Dot and Merry both had full-time jobs. Dot looked after babies in a nursery, and Merry said her job was "hush-hush," and then she winked her left eye. She made us cross our arms over our chests and swear if she let us know what her job was, we would not tell anyone her secret.

We crossed our arms over our chests—and then she shook laughing. "Gotcher!"

I didn't get the joke, nor did Monica. Paula and few of the others laughed, but they couldn't explain it when we asked. That often happened to me with grownup jokes. Viv was always saying, "You have no sense of humour." I thought I probably ought to try to develop one. I'll look in the library, and perhaps I'll find the formula in a book.

Dot and Merry had two vans. They camouflaged both vans themselves with swirly dirty yellow, green, brown, and khaki paint. "You should've seen us when we finished." Merry laughed. "We could've been mistaken for a new secret weapon for the war effort. It took us hours to scrub the paint off. Wouldn't you know there was no electricity, and the water was cut off when we were still dirty."

Crammed inside the vans was the camping gear: one bell tent, one ridge tent, rolled-up blankets, enamel mugs and plates, and a huge aluminium pot for boiling water. Except for the driver's seat, which was fixed, we sat on a motley assortment of imports: old car seats, old cinema chairs, and old cushions.

"All this came from Abe's junk yard down the road," said Dot. "My old dad taught me how to find a bargain. He'd have been proud of me finding this lot for three quid."

Our drive to the farmer's field was reckless. Every bend, every sudden stop, every army lorry we passed going the other way had its effect—we were banged and bounced from side to side, but we didn't care. When we undressed, we proudly shared our bruises, and our remarks hung like a balloon over our heads.

"Mine's bigger than yours."

"Yes. But mine's got more colours."

"If it's purple and on your hip it hurts more."

"My dad was called Bruiser at school. It's a good name for you."

Much had to happen before we saw those bruises. Dot and Merry assigned chores, and we all ran off in different directions. We didn't want the air-raid wardens who patrolled the area to come after us, so we made sure our torches were taped and gave only a slit of light. We went in twos. Two to fetch the water, two to raise the tents and mallet the wooden pegs in the ground, two to scout around for small twigs to start the fire, and two to stow our small rucksacks once the tents were up. Then the fun began. Merry would boil water for our mugs of cocoa and start frying the bangers for lunch. The sausages were mostly made of bread and flavouring, but their burnt outsides, all crispy, made you forget their insides.

"Don't forget to put the spuds in the fire," Dot said. "I managed to find a scrape of margarine for everyone."

"Yum," we said breathily.

And yum it was when we ate those spuds. The hard, crackly skins became a favourite of mine forever, as did the smell of a campfire burning. Our two days were filled. We played Rounders, Cricket, Pig-in-the Middle, Mother May I, Oranges and Lemons, and Kick the Can until we were breathless.

Dot and Merry said we had to rest in our tent, otherwise we'd have no energy to help cook supper, go for a hike around the woods, play charades, and end up with a sing-song. I was exhausted at the thought but happy that charades was on her list. We had played them at home when Grandma Hal and Grandpa Lewis came to visit. My mum was good at acting, and Viv and I were good at guessing. I wondered what words Dot and Merry would want us to act out.

We rested. I was in the bell tent. Merry told us it was a leftover one from the Great War, World War One.

"Her father picked it up at Abe's," said Dot. "Got it for a song."

We started to softly sing all the songs we knew from the First World War. Our list was long. My grandpa Henry fought in the Boer War and WWI, and he would sing all the army songs he knew from those wars before WWII started. He moaned about war and fighting: "They called it 'the war to end all wars,' and look at the mess we're in now." He said that, but I didn't think he was a real pacifist. Not like Uncle Eliezar, who had refused to fight but helped soldiers who were wounded. Some people called him a coward, but I thought he was very brave.

Gillian had a clear soprano voice, and she knew how to harmonize. Kate and I had low voices and tended to wander off-key. Sheila said she couldn't sing, but we knew she could and made her join in. She always would in the end. When we sang "Keep the Home Fires Burning" and "There's a Long, Long Trail." Merry wept and Dot blinked quickly. When Gillian sang "There'll Be Bluebirds over the White Cliffs of Dover," I had a pain in my chest. I wasn't sure if it was the pain of patriotism or of pacifism. All the singing put the rest of the tent to sleep. And we dozed too.

The clubbers from the ridge tent lifted the flap of ours. "Rise and shine, shirkers. Time to cook supper."

Yawns and groans accompanied stretching and limbering. The groans came from tired bodies, not unwilling volunteers. Dot and Merry were able to make every chore fun. That was how our two days passed. Our two nights were spent snuggled in tents, wrapped in two blankets made into envelopes held together by three kilt safety pins. The nights were often scary. Dot told ghost stories. Her stories frightened us. Gillian started crying. We tried to comfort her. Her body shook like jelly.

We heard sirens. They were faint, and we assumed far away. An explosion sounded in the distance. We stayed very quiet. Another explosion sounded nearer and louder.

Aileen peered out of the tent. "It sounds like it fell on the other side of the woods. A long way away."

I realized she was trying to reassure us.

A drone hung heavy in the air. It stopped.

Silence.

The explosion was nearer.

I thought it was at the bottom end of the field.

Aileen said, "Come out now. You can almost see where it fell. It's far and always sounds nearer than it is." We thought we almost saw the hole. We weren't sure. When we discussed how much we'd tell our parents about the bombs, we decided we'd tell only of the games and good times.

"My dad'll never let me come again if I tell him about the missiles," said Joan.

"I can't lie," said Emma, "but I won't say anything unless my mum asks."

Mum and Dad listened to the news and read the papers every day, and I was convinced they would find out about the missiles even though the papers didn't report exact locations. I didn't want any of us to lose the chance of having fun.

I said, "I'm not sure what I'll say. All I know is that camping with you clubbers and laughing with Dot and Merry is the *second* best thing that's happened to me in this whole bloomin' war."

Emma asked, "And what's the first?"

"Coming home. Being with Mum and Dad. And Viv. Nothing will ever be better." As I answered, I closed my eyes and saw Mum smiling, Dad teasing, and Viv brushing mascara on her eyelashes. I saw our dining room and knew what our home smelled of—good cooking.

It was a mix of top-notch British and old Sephardic recipes rolled into one, and the scrumptious smell travelled everywhere. When the war was over I knew we would go places Mum and Dad couldn't take us during the war. I'd read about Fez. I wanted to travel to Morocco and explore the ghetto in Fez. I hoped they would consider taking us there.

My life as a gym clubber and weekend camper gave me friends, games, and the enjoyment of sleeping in a tent and cooking on an open fire. The bonus was getting away from the Vee-ones and Vee-twos.

149

I would never be a serious gymnast, I knew that, but Dot and Merry had given me my confidence back about my body. They told me I had good energy and was a trusted support for the star gymnasts in our class, and that having a broad beam was an advantage.

They would have been kind foster parents. Of that I was sure.

CHAPTER 20

RUNNING THE STREETS

"Mark, you can't let her do it. You can't, and I won't let you. She's too young to be on the streets. Racing around in the dark."

I tried to interrupt, but Mum was going on and on. Dad twiddled his moustache and rubbed the side of his nose and looked at me. I'd badgered Dad whenever I cornered him.

"Go on, Dad. Please, please, pleeeease!"

When Dad winked and whistled at the same time, I knew I had a chance of winning. "You'll make us oldies stand to attention, my girl. I know you've got your heart set on it, but your mum's right. This is not a game. Air raids are not for playing games and being a heroine. We'll worry if you're running around Harvest Road and up the villas to the High Road."

I'd pictured those names many times. When I was in the foster homes, I ached to run on their pavements or play hopscotch outside the doctor's office in Brondesbury Villas.

Since I'd returned to my own home, I knew where the firewatchers' stations were, and I'd drawn my own map of how to get from one to the other. But Dad was right. War was not a game.

Dad had come home after his night on duty and said, "They need a messenger. Someone who can run fast and tell the men at the next station where the fires are."

I shouted excitedly, "I can do it, Dad. I'll be the runner. I'm not a brilliant runner. I'll never be as fast as our cousin Harold Abrahams." I smirked.

Harold Abrahams was an Olympic runner and the first Jew to get a gold medal in the 100 yards. At school, I pretended he was one of our relations. Some of the pupils believed me. Last year one of my favourite teachers whispered to me, "You're not the quickest runner in your age group, Joy, but by golly, you put your heart and soul into it."

"I'll put my heart and soul into it, Dad. I will, Mum. I want to help in the war. All those messages on the walls tell us 'Put your Shoulder to the Wheel' and 'Help the War Effort,' and at school the teachers say we all have to do our best in wartime. I want to do my very best. I do. You ran away to join in the First World War, Dad. You lied and told them you were eighteen. Why can't I pretend I'm a boy and join the army? You said you were only sixteen when you enlisted. Well, I hate not being old enough."

Even as I argued, the thought of fighting and killing felt wrong.

My sister said, "You'll never get in anyway, silly."

I wasn't tall and looked younger than fourteen and didn't have a hope of looking older.

Viv added, and breathed loud enough for me to hear, "Fat chance you'll have."

Dad said he'd talk it over with Mum that night and come up with their answer before school in the morning.

And that's how it happened. They agreed. And I became a "messenger." I had a special tin hat with an M painted on it. In red. The paint had dripped down the stem of the letter M and onto the brim. It looked gory. I had a messenger's pouch that I slung over my left shoulder and across my chest. If there was anything in the pouch, I could hold it tightly to my right side as I ran.

It would make it easier because my gas mask was slung over my right shoulder. We had a dress-up rehearsal. Mum said she wished she had a film for her Brownie Box, but films were impossible to find.

The smile on her face was shaky. "I'll never forget the way you look in your tin hat, Joy. I'll remember you forever."

The night before Dad took me to the station, my sleep was sporadic. *Florence Nightingale, Joan of Arc, Florence Nightingale, Joan of Arc, Florence* ... their names pulsated round and round my mind, and their faces, cut from old magazines and stuck on the walls of our bombed-out school halls, danced before my eyes. Perhaps I would become a heroine—one of the strong women from history books. *It would make up for those three years away,* I thought. I could grow into a different person, emerge from my hiding place and forget about my shadow-living.

I wondered whether someday some schoolgirl would look at my hall photo and tell her friends all the brave things I had done: running to deliver messages, dodging bombs, fighting fires with grownup men. I gave a heavy sigh of satisfaction and fell into a deep sleep.

The night Dad took me to the station, my stomach tingled. The moon played hide and seek with the clouds, and with me. One moment I could see it and the next minute—nothing. When I could see its face in a puddle, I felt happy. I wanted it to follow us all the way there. We reached the firewatchers' place, and I let go of Dad's hand. We sidled into a small opening in the wall.

The noise deafened me. I'd never heard so many orders shouted around.

"Get two over to QP!"

"Four fell at 34 Flint. Two duds."

"Number six can't find the address."

"Pull that bleedin' curtain tight, George."

The tips of cigarettes glowed red, and I couldn't breathe. There was so much old smoke, and I could see only bits and pieces of heads and bodies.

One of the faces grinned. "So. This 'ere's y'r kid, eh Scottie? She c'n pass as a young feller with that tin hat on 'er 'ead. Hope she c'n run as fast as yer told us. Anyways, us buggers can't be choosers."

I'd forgotten Dad's other name. He never used our real surname in the outside world. "Once they know you're Jewish, that's it. No insurance company, no bank, no ad agency. *Nisht.* We're all crooks to them. They still live in the Dark Ages." Dad explained.

When the same man's voice said, "'Allo then, Miss Scott," I answered sprightly, "Hello."

I was ready for action.

My first action night came five nights later. I tied my comfortable old plimsoles in a double bow and ran down Harvest Road. It was cloudy, and I wished there was a moon. When I reached the entrance of HQ, a voice said, "'Ere's the messenger. It's Scotty's kid t'night. C'mon in. Scotty's over there. 'E came 'ere straight from work."

It all looked organized inside, but in the dim light I could see that four men were playing cards in one corner and a tall man was reading in an armchair. I gasped. I realized that man was my own father. He looked so different in his greasy overalls. We hardly had time to talk when the air-raid siren wailed.

"Always happens when I have a handful of royals," the skinny card player said as they threw their cards on the upturned crate.

We gathered round a large map that was stuck on the wall while the chief gave orders. I stood to attention and felt silly.

One of them laughed. "You can stand at ease, little Scotty. We hope you won't have too much to do t'night. It's bin quiet for the last three."

"Don't tempt the gawds, Bill," said Chiefie, "'cos that's when things start to happen."

And they did. The distant gunfire got louder, the thuds and bangs sounded closer, and the telephones began ringing.

"We're needed by the railway station. You three off there now!" And off the card players went.

Chiefie turned to Dad and me. "Church down the road 's aflame. You and little Scottie get down there and see what you can do. Then send her back to let me know. She'll be needed all over the place tonight. Not enough of us. The other stations are trying to tackle things, but I think all hell's broken loose in the southeast. Off you go now!"

And off we went.

It was hard keeping up with Dad's long stride, and as I ran, I wondered, How are we going to put out the fire?

Dad must have read my mind. "Just follow me, my girl. Do as I do and keep close."

Dad had been a Special Constable early on in the war, and he knew what to do in a crisis. I felt safe in a funny kind of way.

"What's that crackling, Dad? Sounds like when kindling is lit, only much louder. Churches aren't built of wood, are they? Christchurch is made of white stone with metal bits in it. Mum told me all the iron railings and metal was melted down at the beginning of the war. So why is there crackling?"

Dad stopped my questions. "Enough chit-chat. We need your arms, not your mouth."

I swallowed the lump in my throat. Dad could be kind and cruel at the same time.

Suddenly his voice changed. It sounded jovial. "Good Alf, I'm glad it's you, mate. You on top of things here? They're worried back at the post, and Chiefie wants our messenger to let him know PDQ."

PDQ was a grown-up phrase. Dad wouldn't let Viv or me use it. There was a swear word in it. Viv said it when he was not home. It meant "pretty damn quick." I said it under my breath when I got impatient.

Alf was growing impatient. "'Sno good, Scotty, water's run out. You and the kid take these buckets and douse out what you can. You c'n fill 'em from the tank over there. We've got to stop the spreading. The others are in there trying to get at the core. The pulpit and screen have almost gone, but it's all them wooden pews that are really taking it."

The buckets were heavy. They were hard to carry and not spill when you were going as quick as you could. It was hot, and the sweat was running down my face. Dad's glasses were all steamed up. He couldn't see without them. We moved slowly toward the end of the church.

Then Dad shouted, "See that space? Those are the steps that lead to the belfry, where they ring the bells. I'll hoist you up and I'll follow. I think we can get to the rafters and stop them burning."

Dad hoisted me up, came after me, and we both scrambled as fast as we could up the stone stairs. I hurt my elbows and knees on the walls. I knew Dad was banging his elbows and knees 'cos he was so tall. The stairs suddenly ended—one way led to the bells and the other to the rafters. We could see them all crisscrossed in triangles.

The rafters were burning. Not huge flames like the pews on fire, but small bursts of flame all mauve and aquamarine.

"Dad, I'll crawl along that beam, and if you pass me a bucket of water, I'll douse that fire there." I pointed to the one nearest us. "I'll test the beam. I'm sure it'll bear my weight."

I started forward, legs astride the beam, before Dad had a chance to say no.

We got into a rhythm—Dad handing me a nearly full bucket of water and me swinging my legs in unison to propel myself forward with my hands holding the bucket on the beam.

Alf's face appeared behind Dad. "The water supply's replenished, Scotty. A miracle! 'Ere's a small hose. It'll be much easier to reach them rafters. You're doin' a good job, young missie. Take care now."

Dad pulled the hose, and I reached for the nozzle and pulled as hard as I could. It hardly budged an inch. I used every ounce of energy I could muster. It moved. I tucked it under my arm and twisted the nozzle open. A trickle of water came out—then a gush—and then a mighty swoosh, and the hose twisted like a snake. The water drenched me. I lost my balance and fell. Down. Down. Down. Dad yelled. I think I screamed. Yes. It was me. I screamed and screamed.

I couldn't close my legs in time. I landed astride a lower rafter and then fell forward.

My whole body hurt. Especially between my legs. There must have been some glass somewhere, because there was blood trickling down.

Dad reached me. He put his arms around me and squeezed me. I felt him shaking. I thought he was crying.

"I'm all right, Dad. I am. Honest. I'm sorry I screamed. I shouldn't've lost my balance. Please don't tell Mum. I'll be all right. I will. I will."

I couldn't tell him where I hurt. We never talked about that part of my body.

Dad fussed over my leg. "Looks like a deep gash. There's a lot of blood. We'd better go back and tell the chief. They have some first-aid equipment at the station, and I'll clean you up. I think the men are getting it under control down below. Alf's blowing his whistle. It's the signal for us to leave. Your Mum'll have to know. You could have broken your back in the fall."

My career as a fire fighter ended. My career as a messenger continued.

I put my heart and soul into running and delivering important messages.

I told no one about the hurt between my legs.

CHAPTER 21
REVEALING SECRETS

Sometimes I wondered whether Mum had second thoughts about sending us away.

I knew what she said on the outside, but what about her inside thoughts?

Viv and I had told Mum how it was in some of the foster homes, but about most of what happened we kept silent.

"Keep a Stiff Upper Lip." "Don't You Know There's a War On?" Those huge signs seemed burrowed in our brains.

One night, when we were singing ourselves to sleep with "Red Sails in the Sunset," Viv whispered, "I'll tell you a secret if you promise not to tell."

"I can't. It may be awful. It could hurt someone if I don't."

"You're such a prig, Joy. Grow up. I'm going to tell you anyway. You ought to know." She told me. I became wide awake. Her story shocked me. I couldn't believe that she had been sent away again and by our own mum and dad. I reached out over the gap between our beds and held her hand. I felt awful. Sick in my belly.

Why hadn't I known? Why hadn't Mum and Dad told me? What was it all about? I knew she had shakes and tics when Mum brought her back to London two years before me. Mum told me I had to stay with the Downeys, but that the Fitzgeralds had been cruel to Viv and she needed to see a doctor in London. I thought those foster parents were stuck-up snobs.

I didn't know how cruel they had been. I had seen bruises on her legs but never knew what had happened. Had I known, I would have banged on their door and whopped Mr. Fitzgerald on the nose.

After she had returned to London, I only heard snippets about what Viv was doing. She didn't answer any of the letters I wrote to her. I tried to forget about her for months.

I was jealous that she had been allowed to come home. I wished I had been ill enough to make Mum and Dad worry.

Now, as she told me what had happened, all those feelings disappeared. I climbed into her bed. We cuddled. I tried to find the words to explain my actions, my immaturity.

After several hours of whispering our feelings about the incidents, we fell asleep. In the morning, my heart felt light. I had a clean slate. Viv and I could start afresh. When I thought about what she had gone through, and the abuse she suffered at the hands of the Fitzgeralds, I knew she was braver than me.

The doctor had told Mum that Viv had lost weight and had facial tics and odd hand and arm movements because she had been under a lot of stress. The doctor said she needed a quiet, peaceful place to be.

"Fat chance to find that in London these days," said Viv.

Dad had asked Mrs. Lovelace if she had room for Viv. He said that a short stay with her would be ideal. Unfortunately, soldiers were billeted at her cottage, but she did recommend a friend who took in paying guests. They agreed to take an unaccompanied teen. Viv said they had three dogs: Bruno, Blacky, and Boris. She petted and played with them all day, and that helped her sleep and to stop shaking her arms. Dad didn't have the money for more than two weeks.

Viv told me he was cross that it cost so much; it took all his savings. He thought she was acting out so she could get her own way. Viv explained, "We argued a lot. Dad said things that often rubbed me the wrong way. I answered him back. He didn't like that. He believed children should be seen and not heard. Dad was so old-fashioned."

When Viv was brought home from the Fitzgeralds, she persuaded Mum and Dad to allow her to drop out of school. "I'm no good in any school subjects, and I've always wanted to work in a hairdresser's."

Abe Miller was a friend of our family who owned a hairdressing salon in the West End. Dad had discussed Viv' school difficulties with him, and he said Viv had shown talent when she assisted the salonista. He agreed to give Viv a contract for one year as an apprentice.

Viv needed me to be her guinea pig for new hairstyles. Every week I had to sit for an hour while she primped and curled my hair. I wasn't very good at sitting still for long times. I would complain, "Haven't you finished yet?!"

Viv would say, "I'm doing you a favour, and you're doing me a favour, so hush up and stop moaning."

The senior salonista's name was Elsie, and I met her when I returned from the Downeys. Elsie lived in Whitechapel, where many Jewish families lived. She was different from many grownups I knew; she was open and funny and warm. She and Viv became close friends, and they allowed me to hang on with them.

Elsie could speak Yiddish fluently and made us laugh when she translated what she quoted. She taught us a few phrases. I liked, "*Az me est chazzer, zol rinnen iber de bord!*" In English it meant, "If you're going to do something wrong, enjoy it!"

Elsie said the Yiddish words were funnier. The exact translation of the Yiddish phrase meant, "Let the grease from eating traif run into your beard!" Viv and I had eaten *traif* (bacon, ham, and pork) when Mrs. Young made us. We knew it was wrong. We felt helpless.

When Viv and Elsie worked in the salon, air raids were frequent, and at night many Londoners took shelter in London underground stations. Viv told me how she and Elsie would take their sleeping bundles to a tube station in a *high-class* area, like St. John's Wood or Swiss Cottage, and leave for work from those stations in the morning. She said they didn't go home until their clothes needed washing. Once they stayed away for three weeks.

"That's when Dad got livid. When I did go home, his face was purple and he spluttered his anger on my dress."

He shouted, "I almost called the police. I came looking for you at Maida Vale, Willesden, Hampstead—all the places I knew you had friends. You're never to sleep down the tube at night again."

Viv continued. "Dad said I was bolshy." I wasn't sure what that meant, so she explained. She said that it came from the Russian word Bolshevik, the political party that became the Communist party in 1918 and who were known for wanting to turn things upside down.

I learned that Dad then asked his sister, our aunty Netty, if Viv could live with her. She reluctantly agreed to do it for a month. It didn't work out. Viv turned her nose up. "She wasn't my favourite aunt. She was too finicky and persnickety. I never did anything the way she thought it ought to be done, not even filling the kettle or wiping the kitchen table. And that Danish au pair was always trying to get me into trouble. She reported everything I did. Uncle was fed up with hearing all the palaver. He went to Dad's work and said I was a troublemaker and they had to take me back."

Daddy made Viv sleep at home from then on. "I tried hard to keep my tongue under control." She grinned.

Her life was with her friend Elsie. They were members of a popular Jewish youth club. Most of the teenagers were socialists, and Elsie told me the atmosphere was democratic. I went there, but the boys were too old for me. All the members flirted. Viv and Elsie fluttered their eyelids and said silly things.

I preferred playing near my home and with our friend Ruth. We both knew her from school. Dad called her his third daughter. We bounced balls together against the side wall of our house. We played tennis in the park. We cycled for miles and miles to faraway villages and small towns. It was another way we could forget about the war.

Our friend had a clever way of helping us be even closer as sisters. She explained how we could help solve our problems by using words to get to the heart of any quarrels that might have started. We called ourselves The Three Sisters, a pub's name in Sussex where Dad would buy us a shandy, before the war.

Dad said he was going to take Mum to Bournemouth for a rest for a couple of weeks. Our family believed the sea air was like strong medicine. "You breathe it in and all your ills get blown away."

I hoped it would do the same for Mum.

"Look after my girls for me," Mum said to Ruth. "Two weeks is a long time." We looked at each other. Not as long as three years, I thought.

We did have happy times. Viv created new recipes and was clever at making something out of nothing. She was like the stranger in the Jewish story of "Stone Soup" who bamboozled villagers into supplying all the real ingredients for a magical soup made from a simple stone. I enjoyed that story and how poverty and hunger had forced the stranger to use his smarts to survive.

We were as active as always, and the time that Mum and Dad were away passed quickly.

We were playing catch in the front garden when we suddenly saw Mum and Dad walking slowly down the street. We opened the gate and ran to meet them. Dad explained that Mum was not feeling well and they had decided to return early.

Mum smiled. Her breath came in short spurts. It frightened us.

We put our arms around her and helped her into our bed-room, where the sun shined. "You and Dad have our room, Mum. The sun will help you—the vitamins'll be good. We'll get some rosehip syrup too, and perfume of the winter jasmine that you love so much will waft in."

Mum smiled weakly.

We had a lady doctor for our family, Dr. Harris. We liked her. Even Dad did. He was impressed with her general knowledge and political savvy. "She's an intelligent lady, and she speaks the King's English."

When he said things like that, I bristled. I reminded him that many people in England had accents. His father's second cousin, Jankel, had a pronounced one. It didn't mean you were unintelligent.

"Now don't you start getting bolshy too, young lady."

Neither of us wanted to start an argument when Mum was ill.

Then an extraordinary thing happened. Dr. Harris came to see Mum in our front bedroom twice. Doctors rarely did that. So we knew it was serious. She called for an ambulance to take Mum to hospital to treat her breathing. "She has an infection in her lungs" she told us soberly.

Dad tried to help us three sisters. "Your mother will get the treatment she needs. She won't be there long."

CHAPTER 22

VE DAY

WWII was officially over on May 8, 1945, when VE Day was declared. VE meant victory in Europe. Everyone in England, and most in Europe, went crazy. Londoners rushed down to Trafalgar Square, Parliament Square, and Buckingham Palace. They wanted to see the king and queen. They wanted to see Winston Churchill with his big fat cigar. And they wanted to celebrate. They didn't mind who they saw, as long as they looked important and were waving from the balcony of the palace.

Viv, Elsie, and I never reached Trafalgar Square or the Palace. We got no further than Piccadilly Circus. By the time we arrived the crowds were too dense. The golden statue of Eros, the god of love, had been boarded up during the war, but there were men and women who had managed to reach the top. They tore down the wood covering it and were clinging on to Eros's body. It looked precarious to me. Policemen tried to haul them down but weren't successful. Everyone was dancing: on the pavement, in the road, on top of parked vehicles; they were climbing and clambering and cheering and whistling. They were swilling beer by the barrel.

The sound was deafening. Strangers were kissing and clasping each other; ages seemed not to matter. I saw a woman with white hair embrace a boy in short pants. Perhaps she was his grandma; it was hard to tell. I liked seeing people happy and hearing their songs, but I didn't want to be pawed by men who stank of beer.

After three hours I said to Viv I wanted to go home. I didn't like crowds bumping into me, but the biggest reason was that Mum had been taken to hospital two days earlier and it felt wrong that I was here and she was there. Viv and Elsie were enjoying themselves. They were flirting with two soldiers who seemed respectful enough, but I hoped they weren't going to get drunk or drag my sister and Elsie off somewhere. Dad had said we all had to stick together, and when I reminded Viv of this, she pulled a long face.

In the end they both agreed to leave. "This corporal's getting too frisky," said Elsie.

"Mine's realized I'm not yet seventeen." Viv laughed.

The crowds were still milling down Regent Street, and it was hard trying to move in the opposite direction. We had to reach Oxford Street and find the Bakerloo line to get home.

Buses had been diverted, and the ones we could see were crammed to capacity.

We did get home. At quarter to three in the morning. Dad was waiting for us in our bedroom. He was cross, but all he said was, "No giggling, girls. We've a busy day tomorrow, shopping and going to see Mum. Let's hope her lungs are in better shape. And remember, the hospital has very strict visiting hours."

CHAPTER 23

HOLE IN THE GROUND

While my mum was in the hospital, Headmistress Dawe had been understanding and given me permission to be absent from school for three afternoons a week.

When I arrived at the hospital, the head nurse let me enter the ward, even though visitors were not allowed during the daytime. She whispered to me, "Make sure Matron doesn't see you. She's a stickler for rules. Talk softly to your mother, don't tire her, and don't stay too long."

During my visit, Mum asked me whether I was still enjoying Latin. Latin translations were very difficult, and I had lousy marks on my homework, but I didn't want to worry her so I said that I liked French better.

Mum leaned forward and whispered, "Learn as many languages as you can. Use them. Travel the world and find out how other people live. It's important. I never had the chance to travel, but now the war's over you'll soon be able to cross the Channel." She kissed me and sat back on her plumped-up pillows with a big smile.

I was happy to leave her smiling, and I went home, had my supper, and dressed for gym. I called on my friend Pat, and we went to class. Our gymnastic routines had to be in shipshape for our upcoming performance in two weeks time. Dot and Mary had said there would be many family and friends coming to see our presentations. We rehearsed our routines for the next two hours. We tumbled and rolled and sprung over the vault-horse. I used so much energy practising that I almost forgot Mum was in the hospital.

When gym class was over, Pat and I cycled home. It was a warm May evening, between dusk and darkness, the kind of evening Dad called balmy. We were both hot, and there was so much more to talk about that we couldn't bear to say good night.

We cycled on our usual route past my house, and then on to hers and back again.

Sitting on the steps of the front door of her house, her father was smoking his pipe. "Last ride!" he shouted.

Pat held up two fingers in a V for victory sign. She cycled back with me to my house.

We sang raucously, bouncing on our saddles in time with the number of my house. "One three one. Here we come. One three one. Here we come."

"Look, Mum. No hands."

We laughed. That was an old joke.

Dad said it when we took our hands off our handlebars and waved our arms in the air. We balanced our bicycles with our knees and wove in and out like a figure eight. Dad worried we might fall and crash into each other. We were confident. We pretended we were trick cyclists.

We stopped to catch our breaths.

Pat knew something was on my mind, and she knew my mother was in the hospital. She asked, "What's the matter with her?"

"I don't know. It's hard to find out. I hope she'll be home soon. Pat, I'm missing so much school. I'll probably fail my matric'. And then what'll I do?" I was cross with myself for thinking about maths. Mum taught us to think of others, and all I was being was selfish and thinking of myself.

I was happy that almost three weeks ago the war in Europe had ended. I wanted it to be over in the Far East as well so that Pat's three cousins could be released from their prisoner-of-war camp in Burma.

"You don't have to worry about exams," Pat said. "You'll sail through. You passed seven subjects in mock matric', and most of our class only passed five. And your Mum'll recover; she's young. I'll pray for her at Mass." Pat's family was Roman Catholic. They prayed hard. I didn't tell her about my fiasco with prayers.

When we reached my side door, I flung my bike against the concrete step. I opened the door and called to Pat, "Won't be a mo'. I'll tell Dad I'm home from gym and then I'll cycle back with you. This'll be the last time tonight."

I pushed our living room door open energetically. Viv held a pencil and paper.

Dad sat at the table. His glasses were smeared. Tears ran down his cheeks.

I took one step forward but couldn't move. I felt glued to the lino.

Everything froze in front of me. My ears were blocked. I heard nothing.

I screamed but no sound came.

Daddy pulled me close and kissed the top of my head. I pulled away.

I couldn't talk. I couldn't cry. I didn't know where to turn, where to put my face.

"No. No," I whispered. "It's not true. It hasn't happened. You're play-acting. It's a charade. Mum's all—"

"Mummy's dead," said Viv, her voice scratchy. "She died after we left this evening. Daddy wants me to make a list of family and friends we should notify. The funeral's at the Ground on Sunday, and we'll be sitting *shiva* at Mr. and Mrs. Lewis's flat."

Shiva is the Jewish custom where family and friends comfort the mourners. Religious people sit *shiva* for seven days.

I knew Viv was trying to be kind. Her voice said so. But nothing helped. I sank to the floor and stuck my fingers in my ears. I gulped some air. I sobbed softly. I don't know how long I stayed there. My hearing gradually came back as I listened to Viv's list. I felt sick at the thought of going to the funeral. I'd never been to one. I had been to the Ground—our synagogue's cemetery—but that was with Mum, and now I would be going *for* Mum.

We used to go as a family every Yom Tov to remember our great-grandparents who were buried there. Before the war, when we were little, we played hide-and-seek between the tombstones until Dad told us off.

"Show some respect, girls. These are your ancestors. Great-Uncle Moses doesn't want his peace disturbed." Dad could be cross and funny at the same time. I thought of the tombstones. I thought of Pat. Was she still outside holding my bicycle? I didn't want to see her now.

I heard a clatter from the hallway. A voice shouted, "Your bike's there, Joy."

I didn't feel brave enough to go to the Ground for my Mum. What will I do when I see her coffin and know that she's in it? How can I say good-bye to her, my dearest darling mother? I can't. It's not fair. Why did she die? I'll refuse to go. Will Dad force me? And if he does, and I have to go, what'll I wear? I haven't got any black clothes. Neither does Viv. I won't know what to do at the *shiva*.

Viv answered my questions before the words came out of my mouth. "We'd better get some sleep. There'll be things to do in the morning. I have to go next door and ask Mrs. Sofaer if we can use her phone. Dad wants me to let Uncle Sidney and Aunt Kate know, though he says he hasn't seen them for years."

Aunt Kate gave me my first dictionary: Oxford University. I was proud to have a dictionary of my own. Last year I had asked Dad why we had stopped going to Uncle Sidney and Aunt Kate's cottage. He explained that she had said cruel things to Viv, had told her she was stupid and wouldn't amount to anything.

"Your mother and I wouldn't put up with that and we told her so. She's always had a sharp tongue."

I wished Aunt Kate could see Viv now. She was acting so grown up, and Dad was letting her make all the decisions. Dad asked us to sleep together in one twin bed and he would sleep in the other. The three of us cried ourselves to sleep.

The next seven days were a nightmare. They either felt like seven years or seven minutes. Time collapsed and expanded, collapsed and expanded. Family members sent telegrams, so the postman was banging on the front door at all hours. Our non-Jewish friends sent flowers, and we didn't have enough vases. The scullery sink was full of blossoms and pussy willows.

Mrs. Sofaer cooked a *cholent*, a traditional Jewish stew. "You've never tasted one as good as mine," she said.

We didn't mind her boasting. She was a real *balabusta*. She gave me a spoonful of her potato and meat *cholent* one winter. It was like Mum's stew but had twice as many potatoes. Dad said it was kind of her to bring food. She brought us messages from family who had been telephoning us at her number. We didn't have our own phone. In wartime you couldn't have a phone unless you were important. We weren't.

Aunty Netty and Uncle Leon came to our house with their two dogs, Poppy and Butch. Poppy had a curly coat, wagged his tail vigorously, and rolled over when we scratched his back. Scratching his back helped both of us give teary smiles.

Aunty Netty offered, "You can come and stay at Suntop with me, if you like."

We wouldn't go. We wouldn't leave Dad. We wanted to be with each other.

Uncle Leon sounded serious as he spoke to Dad. "You know, Mark, I went to the hospital and saw Rae. Before she died, she told me she wanted the girls to choose Jewish husbands. That was her wish. She told me it was important to her."

Dad was so upset by Mum's death, nothing further was said, and Leon, Netty, and their dogs kissed us and left.

At the funeral we stood in front of our family and friends—a large crowd dressed in black. I had to hold on tight to Viv's hand. I thought of jumping right in the hole where the men lowered the coffin. The rabbi told us all to take a clump of earth and throw it on top of the coffin. Dad did. Viv did. I took the squeaky clay earth in my hand and mashed it around into a tight ball.

I wanted to throw it at the rabbi. I wanted to hit him hard.

"Why did he ask me to do such a horrid thing?" I was blubbering away.

The sun was strong, and the black dress I had borrowed was sticking to me.

Cousin Julie led me away. I sat on a tombstone in the shade, wrung out my sodden hanky, and waited until Viv and Dad collected me.

As soon as they heard about Mum, the Lewises offered their flat for us to sit *shiva*.

Mum and Dad had played bridge every two weeks with the Lewises. I would visit and watch them play. Mr. Lewis was an expert bridge player. He knew every convention. He had an excellent memory and never forgot which cards had been played.

Last year my parents and the Lewises spent a weekend together at Margate, and they had planned to travel to Paris next year. Mum had been thrilled at the possibility.

Dad and Viv told me we would be saying prayers at their flat for two days. I was relieved. I wasn't sure if I could last seven days. I was glad to get away from the cemetery.

As we were leaving Mum's grave, we came face to face with a large crowd of men and women dressed in black. The women wore enormous black hats decorated with red cherries and multi-coloured flowers. Theirs was three times the size of our funeral group.

Dad's second cousin, Pokey, was walking beside me. "A bigwig bit the dust," he said.

I could see Dad was cross at Pokey's comment, but a watery smile escaped me.

Two funeral cars were waiting for us. We rode in the first one. It was black inside and out and smelled of polished leather. Viv and I sat in the back with Dad, and the men in black drove us from the cemetery to the Lewis's flat. When we arrived it was crowded. I expected some people must have known a shortcut from the Ground. There wasn't a spare inch on the dining table. Eggs and chopped herring. Lox and challah. Poppy seed and apple strudel. There were foods I'd never seen before. Mr. Lewis had been born in Riga, and he made Mrs. Lewis bake the cakes his mother used to make. She didn't mind. Everyone was eating or drinking tea or schnapps. I couldn't. I didn't want to eat. Never again. And if anyone else told me "I'll get over it," that "Time will heal," I felt I would scream in his or her face. I was kissed and patted, hugged and squeezed until I felt grubby. I slunk away into a corner and tried to hide under the table, but Viv hauled me out. She reminded me of what I already knew—that every single member of Mr. Lewis's family had been sent to concentration camps and none had survived. Having *shiva* in his home was a horrible reminder for him.

If England had been invaded by the Germans, would we have been put in camps?

Most of our friends and family were Jewish.

I felt ashamed.

When it was time for prayers, I didn't know enough Hebrew to join in, but all the men and some of the women did. Dad explained to us that the prayers that were chanted during *shiva* celebrated life. I could only think of death, but when they started praying in Hebrew it was soothing. I was so tired that I curled up, fell asleep, and woke up when it was time to go home.

That night everything was rolling around in my head. I tossed, turned, and tried to replay the stories Mum had told me. I started with our talks in the hospital; her voice sounded like an echo: "Promise me you'll marry ..." Then Mum stopped and said, "Viv has St. Vitas Dance, they ..." I felt the tears on her cheeks. They were my tears, my own tears streaking down my cheeks. Mum's voice became jumbled. Bits of one conversation were cut off and tacked onto the beginning of others. "Be careful of that house, dear ... I hope one day ... never believe ... no!" Everything was mixed up. I wanted so badly to hear Mum's real voice, her usual voice, but it wouldn't come. I wanted to see her face and tried hard but saw nothing.

I sang to myself her favourite song, "Poor Butterfly." Mum used to play it on our upright piano. It came from an opera about a Japanese lady. We both cried when Mum played it and I sang. I remembered her fingers playing the black and white notes. I kissed her stubby fingers.

I didn't want them to tire from playing.

Dad brought Mum's bed jacket home from the hospital. Mum's smell was embedded in every lacy stitch. I smothered it over my nose and gently stroked my eyes with its soft fleece. That night, the only way I could get to sleep was by cuddling its memories. I called it Maddy. It was as close to saying "Mum" as I wanted get. It was all too painful. Viv understood. She tucked Maddy under my pillow every night.

I couldn't sleep without her.

Mum died on May 25, 1945. Seventeen days after VE day.

I had an idea that I thought was going to help Viv and me. Mum had a remnants bag in which she kept pieces of material that she loved and admired. She used them when she had a notion about what she was going to sew. Viv and I loved to play with the pieces and drape them over ourselves. I knew what I was going to do with those pieces, and I was sure they would make a difference to us.

When we were in foster homes, there were songs that were played on the wireless that made us cry at night. They were sung by Vera Lynn, a popular singer who entertained soldiers in England and abroad and tried to help everyone be cheerful.

"Goodnight Children" felt directed to Viv and me:

"Goodnight children everywhere,
Your mommy thinks of you tonight
Lay your head upon your pillow
Don't be a kid or a weeping willow
Though you are far away
She's with you night and day
Goodnight children everywhere."

Mum's piano stool was her sheet music's home. I had cut the photo of Vera Lynn, my most favourite singer, out of the newspaper and laid it inside the stool on top of Mum's music.

My idea was to fold her song "Poor Butterfly," place Vera Lynn's photo inside it, put them both on my favourite circle of fabric, and roll them together like scrolls.

Viv liked the idea, and we spent a long time choosing the fabric that felt ideal. I chose a circle with dandelion seeds flying around. Viv found a triangular remnant with strongly defined multi-coloured crosshatched lines. That way, our mum and things dear to her would always be with us. Right under our heads as we slept.

———

In the weeks that followed, I wished my thoughts weren't in a constant muddle. They cross-talked—was I an assimilated Jew, a religious Jew, or no Jew at all?

Why had the war turned me into a non-believer? Had anti-Semitism and bigotry tied me in knots? Why had faith left me?

The mixed beliefs tossed and tumbled in my head and body. Would my feelings be clearer if I wrote them?

Viv discovered me lying on her bed as I puzzled ideas into a notebook. Writing helped.

Viv questioned, raising one eyebrow, "What's in the notebook?"

"I'm trying to sort things out, Viv. I know you can help me. Be serious. What does it mean to be a Jew?"

"Hah! It'll take a lifetime to tell you, Sis. The rabbis try daily, and as they don't seem successful, I doubt I'll be. Accept the fact that you're a Jew and that everyone hates you." Her tone was strong, and its emphasis brought back the years of hearing Jew-hate.

Viv took my pencil and scratched the Star of David on her forehead. Did she think that would protect her? "I have an idea." Her voice quickened. "Let's make a list of the lousy names we've been called in every stinky place."

The list played before my eyes: Kikes, Jew girls, Yiddle Piddle, Christkillers— heard at school, in parks, in billets, where we had pretended we were not hurt by their hateful name calling.

To kids who teased us, Dad told us to recite, "Sticks and stones may bruise my bones but names will never hurt me." That meaning was clear.

Following days of tears, I believed I was no longer myself. Imperceptibly, I had become a copy out of focus. Was this what happened when you grew up?

The day I went back to school, my history teacher snapped, "You're still in mourning, girl? Get over it. It's been seven days. Mona's mother passed the same week, and she's not weeping her eyes out."

I wept more, flabbergasted by her coldness and lack of feeling. I needed the answer to a deeper question. I'd never heard Mum tell us to marry in, or out.

What did it mean to be *in* or *out*? Or *out* or *in*?

I asked Viv whether she thought Uncle Leon had lied about Mum's wish when he had visited her at the hospital.

"I don't know," she answered. "Who can say what Mum's wishes were? You know Uncle Leon, the 'great brain'—trying to impress us with his long words and obscure ideas. He likes to get a rise out of the family. He knows it annoys Dad."

I wasn't sure what to think. I was still so upset and mixed up. What was my Mum's wish?

Mum and Dad had been strict with Viv but more lenient with me. Mum had allowed me to make decisions: what I read, where I went, who could be my friends. She would have given me the opportunity to choose whom I wanted to marry. Viv was seventeen; I was fifteen, and marriage was too far into the future for us. To think about the idea made us both laugh.

Viv said she might marry if she met the right man, but I had plans to travel the world and learn languages.

Mum's death had turned our world upside down. Without Mum, we were both fearful of disappointing Dad and imagined his melancholic expression if we made the wrong choices.

Would we be Jewish if we married out? Would the world around us call us names? After loving us in a marriage, would our husbands turn around and call us "dirty Jews" one day?

Everything that had happened to me strengthened my understanding of what it meant to be a Jew. I whispered and vowed, "I can't predict what will happen, Mum, but I promise to continue searching. Your wish is safely sealed." I knew Mum heard.

I looked at Viv, my fashionable sister. Her dark curled hair fell gently on her shoulders.

She was so grown up. She had protected me from bullies at times when our lives were miserable and difficult, and with clever words and humour she had helped me laugh. Together we had survived, but at what cost? Did our experiences damage us? Would we ever know?

I wondered what would happen if our circumstances changed. If one us impulsively travelled abroad when the opportunity for a new career arose, would we be able to resist the attractions of men, Jewish or non-Jewish? If one of us fell in love and *married out,* how would it affect our relationship with our father? And with each other? Would it change how we felt? Would it tear us apart?

Nothing, not even death, could do that. There was a bond between us: an unbreakable bond that was etched on our hearts.

Not only did we share our love, we shared our mum. We would never let her go.

Perhaps someday we would forget the war, our billets and foster parents, the kindness and unkindness, and the pain of separation. But I knew that these were the shards that cut and shaped us and profoundly influenced my sister and me into the women we would become. Everything that came into our lives left impressions that would never leave us. Their embodiment lives with me.

Forever.

ABOUT THE AUTHOR

 Joy Ruth Mickelson was born in London and is a poet and author of non-fiction and narrative research. *Facing the Shards* is her second book. Her first book, *Our Sons Were Labeled Behavior Disordered: Here is the Story of Our Lives,* was published in the year 2000. Joy Ruth is a member of the Canadian Authors Association, the Writers Guild of Alberta, and the Stroll of Poets Society. As an adjunct Assistant Professor at the University of Alberta, her interest in narrative inquiry continues. She currently lives with her husband Ed in Edmonton, Alberta, Canada.

Made in the USA
San Bernardino, CA
05 September 2016